Your Towns and Cities

Cambridge
in the Great War

Dedication

Dedicated to fond memories of Cambridge, to my sister, Troy Hoskin, who allowed me the run of her home and hospitality while I was researching this book, and to all the people of Cambridge town, gown, and county who fought so valiantly in the Great War on all Fronts, especially to those who made the supreme sacrifice.

'Stands the Church clock at ten to three
and is there honey still for tea?'

(Rupert Brook, Cambridge, 1912)

Your Towns and Cities in the Great War

Cambridge
in the Great War

Glynis Cooper

Pen & Sword
MILITARY

First published in 2016 by
Pen and Sword Military

An imprint of
Pen & Sword Books Ltd
47 Church Street
Barnsley
South Yorkshire
S70 2AS

ISBN 978 1 47383 402 6

A CIP catalogue record for this book is available from the British Library

Printed and bound in England
By CPI Group (UK) Ltd, Croydon, CR0 4YY

Pen & Sword Books Ltd incorporates the Imprints of Pen & Sword Aviation, Pen &
Sword Family History, Pen & Sword Maritime, Pen & Sword Military, Pen & Sword
Discovery, Pen & Sword Politics, Pen & Sword Atlas, Pen & Sword Archaeology,
Wharncliffe Local History, Wharncliffe True Crime, Wharncliffe Transport, Pen &
Sword Select, Pen & Sword Military Classics, Leo Cooper, The Praetorian Press,
Claymore Press, Remember When, Seaforth Publishing and Frontline Publishing

For a complete list of Pen & Sword titles please contact
PEN & SWORD BOOKS LIMITED
47 Church Street, Barnsley, South Yorkshire, S70 2AS, England
E-mail: enquiries@pen-and-sword.co.uk
Website: www.pen-and-sword.co.uk

Contents

Acknowledgements

I would like to acknowledge the help and encouragement I have received in writing this book from family and friends, from Chris Jakes and Celia Tyler at Cambridge Central Library, from local Cambridge historian Mike Petty, and from Roni Wilkinson and the editorial team at Pen & Sword.

Introduction

Cambridge is a major university city and county town in the middle of a large rural area and sometimes difficult to define because there are three main elements to it: town, gown (as the university is colloquially known) and county. In the twenty-first century, a fourth element was added: that of tourism, although this latter element was not really recognisable until the early 1970s. In 1914 it was simply town, gown and county.

The modern town of Cambridge can be traced back to at least AD875 and in medieval times there were leather and woollen industries. It was also an important market and administrative centre with its own mint and a castle by the time of the Domesday Survey in 1086. In 1209, Oxford scholars, seeking refuge from hostile townspeople there, settled in Cambridge, and Peterhouse, the oldest of the Cambridge colleges, was founded in 1284. The original students were only in their mid-teens and caused a fair amount of trouble in the city, but there has always been a certain amount of friction between town and gown, although the university has provided the main 'industry' for Cambridge over several hundred years.

Agricultural production and the country crafts of the villages in the county always found an outlet through the demands of the town and university so that the three main elements were closely linked. In past centuries, much of the town's surrounding countryside was either fenland or swampy marshes, like those of the Wash, in which King John famously lost the crown jewels, and transport was mostly by waterway. A writer of 1654 noted that 'Cambridge is situated in a low-lying and dirty place ... the streets are badly paved ... and the air is infected by the fens', and towards the end of the seventeenth century, Celia

Fiennes, an intrepid traveller, wrote that 'Cambridge lies in a valley with marshy ground around it ... willows surround the town ... the buildings are indifferent and the streets are narrow'.

By the time the First World War began, much of the fen-and swamp-land had been drained. Roads and railways provided quicker means of transport, and effectively linked Cambridge to London. In 1914, much of Cambridge life and trade was centred on the university, although there was a new burgeoning industry of making scientific instruments. The university had its own internal authority, the town had a borough council and the shire had a county council shared with the nearby Isle of Ely. The borough and county councils often collaborated on the maintenance of roads, rivers and sewage works, and also in some health matters.

However, this book will focus mainly on the city of Cambridge, encompassing the town and gown elements. Cambridgeshire and the Isle of Ely will remain peripheral because, while they offered tremendous back-up support and they deserve their own story to be told, it was the city which became the great focus for military, medical and mercantile interests within all the eastern counties during the years 1914–1918, and the university also gave much in terms of man-power, back-up support and war-aid.

CHAPTER 1

1914

It was the middle of the long summer vacation (known locally as the long vac) for Cambridge University. Most students had gone home or on holiday and both landlords and colleges were taking advantage of the opportunity to do some maintenance work, a spot of decorating, or a little DIY. There were summer visitors in the city, but not in overwhelming numbers. They enjoyed boat trips on the river and walking around the colleges, admiring the hallowed halls of learning, even the Gothic splendours of King's College chapel, which D.H. Lawrence was to label so unkindly in the years after the war as resembling an upturned sow. Folk in the city, both town and gown, were aware of the political unrest in Europe. They, like the Cambridge Territorials, wondered about the various military manoeuvres that had been taking place in the East Anglian countryside for the previous five years or so, culminating in a show of strength in 1912. Despite assurances that these were just routine training exercises, many were not convinced and there was much local unease. The fourth day of August 1914 was a gloomy bank holiday with the English weather putting a dampener on local fairs, fêtes and festivals. In Cambridge the Mammoth Show promised 'a bank holiday spectacle of "fancy", horticulture and sport', despite the lack of summer sunshine. Thousands turned out to enjoy an afternoon of entertainment and fun to try and take their minds off more serious matters, but instead the authorities took the decision to announce the declaration of war with Germany at the show. The local paper reported widespread shock, but not surprise, and the 'ending of a weekend of brooding anxiety, especially for the Territorials'.

After that, things happened quickly. The next day, 5 August, the Territorials were mobilised and a sentry was posted at their headquarters in Corn Exchange Street. Army reservists were posted to their depots and outlying Territorials trooped in. On Friday, 7 August, the Yeomanry contingent left Cambridge to join their own headquarters, and on Saturday the Territorials went to Romford for a large gathering of Territorial troops. The Cambridgeshire Regiment, which at that time had only one battalion, began a recruiting campaign that proved to be immediately successful. Eaden Lilley, one of the largest stores in the city, began closing at lunchtime for an hour due to the number of assistants enlisting. County football match competitions were badly affected.

Cambridge has a number of open green spaces or commons such as Midsummer Common, Jesus Green, Lammas Ground, Stourbridge Common and, probably the largest of all, Parkers Piece close to the city centre. The military authorities therefore decided that the town should become a huge army camp for about three weeks while troops were training and resources assessed. Friday, 14 August saw a large concentration of the 6th Division West Yorkshires and Durham Light infantry bivouacked on Butt Green before pitching tents on Midsummer Common and Jesus Green. Infantry filled Midsummer Common, Coldham Common and several adjoining fields. Artillery – horses, men and field-guns – parked on Stourbridge Common. There were troops on Parker's Piece, Donkey's Common, Lammas Ground (at Newnham), while the Royal Army Medical Corps occupied Coe Fen, and the Divisional Cavalry were picketed on Long Common. Army Service Corps stations were set-up on Cherryhinton Road (Cherryhinton is the First World War spelling of the name, today it is spelt Cherry Hinton), while Howitzers and heavy field-gun units were stored on the polo ground at Trumpington. The troops were kept occupied by daily exercises and long marches through the countryside, where they received a cordial welcome from the outlying villages. In the city recreation tents were erected and entertainments

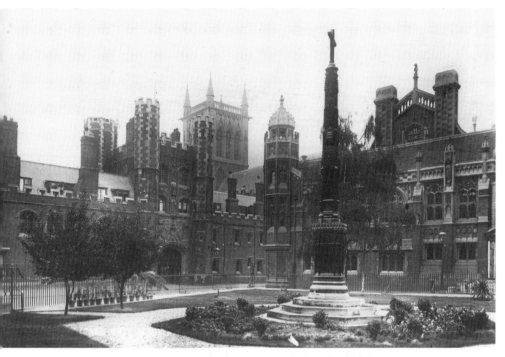

St John's Divinity School c1908

provided, and hospitality was given to everyone. Cambridge, both town and gown, professed themselves 'profoundly moved' by all of these war preparations.

On 7 September, the troops left Cambridge. They marched to a railway enclosure just off Tenison Road, where they boarded the troop trains. Cheering crowds lined the route. Hands were held out to the departing soldiers and gifts given. It was, as one journalist noted, 'a spectacle of girls, cheers and tears'. They waved as the troop trains crossed the Midland Yard and disappeared from view. Next stop would be the Battle of Mons.

The university (gown) was not slow to respond to the situation either. Undergraduates and postgraduates and those about to come up to university volunteered to serve in the armed forces. Cadets and ex-cadets of the University Officers Training Corps received commissions in various branches of the services. During the first eighteen months of the war, almost 3,500 applications were made by members of the university to join the forces and, of these, 2,500 were 'gazetted' to the service for which they had applied, while others obtained commissions in Special Reserve or Territorial forces. University members were also engaged in special war work and administrative duties for the government. In mid-September, it was decided that Cambridge should become a military training centre. Schools, colleges and houses were wanted for billets. Initially military recruits were allowed to occupy Melbourne Place buildings and this was hailed as 'a tribute, to the university public spirit'. Emmanuel College gave the displaced girls' school extra classrooms close to Parker's Piece and, nearby, St Andrew's School agreed to take overflow. Inter-cessionary services were held in Cambridge churches and, though at this stage it was believed that the war would be over in six months, there was intensive recruiting for Lord Kitchener's army and an application for a county regiment. A rural league recruiting scheme was also set-up for the villages. Doctors offered free medical services to the wives and families of all those called-up. An athletes' volunteer force was formed for all sportsmen of any discipline to begin shooting and drilling in their spare time for initial home defence to be followed by national defence, and a Cambridge civilian drill and rifle club was to be set-up. The outer suburban areas of Chesterton and Cherryhinton subsequently formed additional companies in connection with the new Civilian Rifle Corps. Primrose League members began working for the Red Cross and the St John's Ambulance Brigade. The Primrose League, founded in 1883 to promote the aims of the Conservative Party, had taken as its emblem the primrose, which was the favourite flower of Benjamin Disraeli, a former Conservative prime minister. Local suffragettes also offered their services to the Red Cross and there was talk of Cambridge becoming a central medical base for the eastern region of England.

Shortly after the declaration of war, the Aliens Registration Order 1914 came into force. Under its terms those of extraction from countries who were now the enemy had to abide by the following conditions:

- Embarkation or landing was denied to aliens at all except fifteen ports, which included London, Liverpool and Bristol.
- All aliens needed permits to enter or leave the country. They were not allowed firearms or wireless, telephones, carrier or homing pigeons, cars, motorbikes, planes or cipher codes.
- Aliens were ordered to live in specified areas and some districts were prohibited.
- No German, Austrian or Hungarian could travel more than 5 miles from their registered address without a special permit. They were forbidden port areas.
- Failure to report under these conditions and restrictions was a fine of £100 (£8,600) or six months imprisonment.
- Arrival or departure of any foreigner in hotels or lodging houses to be reported to police.

*Members of 11th Battalion of Suffolk Regiment, formed Cambridge 1914
(courtesy of Cambridge Local Studies)*

German women, however, 'on whom no suspicion rests', would not be detained but they had to register and secure travel permits if they left the place in which they lived beyond the 5 mile radius specified. Anti-German feeling ran high, however, and, although the university had some foreign students, a man believed to be a German national was forcibly removed from Corpus Christi College. The Defence of the Realm Act (DORA) was passed on the same day, 8 August, giving the government wide-ranging powers for the period of the war. They could requisition land, buildings, vehicles, horses, food and resources necessary for the war and enforce censorship on journalists, letter-writers and public speakers. Those who opposed the war, like the well-known philosopher Bertrand Russell, were sent to prison. There were lesser restrictions imposed as well, including a ban on flying kites, starting bonfires, buying binoculars and feeding bread to wild animals.

The advent of war had an immediate and unexpected effect on Cambridge. Cambridge didn't have industries like other towns. Its own special industry was the university, which was badly hit by the number of university members signing up to the forces. Lodging houses were the first casualty for they had no students during the summer and now only half the expected number would be coming up for the Michaelmas term due to start in October. This had a knock-on effect for other trades. Building contracts were cancelled or postponed, and so was maintenance and repair work, which resulted in painters, masons and plasterers becoming unemployed. To try and help, the university began to consider certain extension works that would give employment to some of those affected. The printing, bookselling and bookbinding trades were also hit hard. Trade circulars and advertisement printing stopped, accounts were left unpaid, there was a greater economy practised in the buying or ordering of books, and requests for the binding of periodicals declined dramatically. The lack of university trade also affected women's clothing outfitters, tailors and bootmakers, as well as small local laundries.

Lodging house-keepers were the worst affected, however, because they still had to pay rents to the landlords who owned the lodging houses despite the lack of students. Rents were often raised by landlords at the beginning of the new academic year and, despite the war with its resulting effects on the local economy, many saw no reason not to raise the rents as usual. This also happened with the renting of private houses. Many families, whose main breadwinners had gone to war, found themselves having to give up their homes and move in with others, resulting in chronic overcrowding and numbers of empty houses. Inspite of government assurances to the contrary, food prices also began to rise.

The purchasing power of £1 in 1914 was equivalent to £86 in 2015. In 1914, there were 240 old pence (twenty shillings) to the pound. In 2015, there are 100 new pence to the pound. Therefore, one old pence in 1914 was worth around 35 new pence in 2015. So when flour rose by two old pence (2d) per pound (500g) in 1914, it went up by 70p at modern values. Eggs were nine for a shilling (12d), so the cost in modern terms was £4.20. Bacon was £4.90 per 500g, butter was £5.25 per 500g, cheese was £3.33 per 500g, and bread was £2.10 for a large loaf weighing about 1.8kg. Oats were in short supply, although potatoes were said to be plentiful. As food prices began to rise, Hornimans ran a number of adverts which declared that the price of their tea would remain the same despite the war.

Most wages were low. Agricultural labourers, for instance, earned about £1.5s.0d (£107.50), and this amount had to cover rent, food and clothing as a minimum. Trainee soldiers received a guinea (£1.1s.0d) per week (£90.30), and although it rose when they were on active service, their wage was still lower than in many other occupations.

The decision to billet troops for training in Cambridge was welcomed as it alleviated some of the problems caused by the sudden decline in numbers of university men and women. Tailors gained some extra work making officers' uniforms. Military orders also made up a deficit in the bootmaking industry, although there was a shortage of patent leather and French calf materials.

Scientific instrument-making was in demand as well for military purposes, although enlistment meant a shortage of skilled workers. The Primrose League was instrumental in pioneering a new British toy-making industry in various towns including Cambridge, since

Corpus Christi College, WW1 (courtesy of Cambridge Local Studies)

many of the toys bought pre-war were German in origin. The Pitt Press suffered badly.

However, troops spent their hard-earned wages in the town, mostly on drink and entertainment. But this backfired when local publicans were forced to close by 9pm because of the high numbers of military personnel in the town. Barley was used for making bread as well as for beer, and there was some general shortage of grain.

There was an allowance paid for feeding soldiers billeted in private households and they certainly ate well. The recommended breakfast was either macaroni cheese or Welsh rarebit (cheese on toast), sardines on toast or scrambled eggs, maybe a couple of chops, followed by homemade cake and jam plus quantities of tea. The main meal would be meat and two or three vegetables followed by a substantial pudding, such as suet dumplings with syrup or jam roll and custard. This was in great contrast with those on the front line who made do with bully beef (corned beef) and plain dry biscuits, or a helping of Maconochie's stew rations, which was said by many to be 'a culinary abomination'.

To help with the extra work of feeding the troops, 'day girls' were often employed. These girls came from a large pool of unemployed servants. Wealthier citizens were employing fewer servants for reasons of economy, although this increased the workload for those servants who remained in employment and their wages did not increase with the extra hours of work. To some extent the immediate economic impact of the war was cushioned by the town being adopted as both a military training and a medical centre.

By the end of September, 200 wounded soldiers had already been sent to Cambridge for medical treatment and it had been officially decided that the city should become a major military hospital base for the eastern counties. Addenbrookes Hospital, founded in 1766 and still on Trumpington Street in 1914, was a large hospital but totally unable to cope with the numbers of wounded who would be arriving. Temporary wards were erected in Neville's Court at Trinity College, but on 17 September, building work began on a huge hospital complex on land belonging to King's College and Clare College, which had previously been used for cricket matches. Today the university library stands on the former site, just off West Road. There were a number of long narrow wooden huts in neat rows, which held operating theatres, medical buildings and up to 1,700 beds. The complex also included a post office, a shop, a cinema and various recreational facilities. Someone at the time remarked that it was like a small village.

The hospital's full title was First Eastern General Hospital (Territorial Force), but it was known simply as First Eastern. The hospital had some open-air wards using direct sunlight and salt baths to assist in curative treatment. Nurses and medical staff were accommodated locally in vacant college rooms. Red Cross hospitals were also to be set-up to assist, and isolation hospitals were built on Cherryhinton Road and at Barnwell for those suffering from infectious or sexually transmitted diseases.

In October, the first Belgian refugees began to arrive and towards the end of the month, 100 from around Antwerp and Ostend were welcomed to the town. Women and children were accommodated in the Lion Hotel while the men were housed in classrooms adjoining Emmanuel Congregational Church. There was a meeting of representatives from town, gown and countryside to discuss the question of housing the Belgian refugees and providing hospitality, and the university decided to offer sanctuary to academics fleeing from Belgian universities attacked by the Germans. Consequently, the University of Louvain was invited to 'migrate' to the University of Cambridge after the Germans had killed the university rector and destroyed its library of 230,000

Addenbrookes Hospital alterations 1914
(courtesy of Cambridge Local Studies)

Addenbrookes Hospital, Trumpington Street, Cambridge c1912

volumes, including more than 1,000 books printed before 1501. It was finally agreed that the Belgian refugees should be housed in private dwellings in the town or placed with families in the countryside. The village of Duxford was especially keen to help and offered initial places of accommodation for periods of up to thirteen weeks. A Belgian 'badge day' was held in town and county to raise funds for feeding and clothing the refugees, and £600 (£51,600) was collected. As one writer of the day put it, town, gown and county were 'playing their part in this war with gallantry, patriotism and generosity which does honour and credit to its citizens and that all classes are participating in this glorious work is shown by the collection of £600 (£51,600) in the streets on Belgian Badge Day'. By mid-November, a total of 275 Belgian refugees were enjoying hospitality in the county and more again in the town. There were also general offers of hospitality for another 170 Belgian refugees. One hundred and eleven Belgian soldiers arrived on the Red Cross trains for treatment at First Eastern hospital and brought with them unbelievable horror stories of death and destruction. For many Belgians there was an initial language difficulty, but most of them managed to learn English at a basic level fairly quickly. Their tales of the atrocities and scorched earth policy inflicted on Belgium by the Germans shocked their English hosts and army officials. One Belgian barrister was so traumatised that he regarded every single German as a spy and could not understand why all Germans in England were not locked up, even those who simply had German names and whose families had lived in England for generations. At the end of November, a Belgian fête day was held in honour of the fête day of the King of the Belgians (Albert I). Fête day celebrations were also held in other Belgian refugee centres and towns in England and raised more much-needed funds.

However, as Christmas approached, some of the trades connected with the university struggled. There were 1,800 fewer undergraduates and post-graduates in the town, which especially affected the luxury trades and outfitters catering for 'freshers' (those coming up to university for the first time). Although the military and the wounded had brought trade to the town, it was not to these types of businesses. It was, however, the lodging house-keepers who were still the worst affected, despite the need for troop billets. In January 1914 there were just over 770 lodging houses containing 1,930 sets of rooms all of which were occupied. By November 1914, 323 lodging houses had 480 sets of rooms full, while the remaining 450 or so had 1,490 sets of rooms empty.

Economics were to the fore and this war was appearing to be fought on economic principles as much as moral principles, something David Lloyd George understood in the early days of fighting. Huge amounts of money and resources were required to fund the hostilities, and Lloyd George was angered when he discovered that more was being spent on drink in England than on ammunition for the troops. Meanwhile, there was much talk of the war creating unique opportunities for the British textile, metal and sugar trades; and there was a good deal of support

Cambridge Round Church c1907

for a systematic campaign to take advantage of these opportunities, to the extent that the Germans accused the British of insincere concern for the Belgians in order to cover the real British motive for the war, which was envy of German trade and commerce and a desire to rid themselves of this competition.

There were Christmas shopping advertisements in the newspapers alongside continuing advertisements for recruitment, and the New Theatre put on a Christmas pantomime of *Sinbad the Sailor*, but the emphasis this Christmas was firmly on the troops. Employers were asked if they had encouraged all their fit employees to enlist by offering to keep their jobs open and perhaps giving some financial support to their families. Members of the Welsh division of the Territorials were billeted in the town, provoking debate on how to provide for 'their spiritual and social welfare'. In the Guildhall the boy scouts entertained 450 sons and brothers aged 9–14 of serving soldiers and sailors, and the Red Cross held a badge day for wounded soldiers raising £260 (£22,360).

Round Church, Cambridge c1914

Christmas gifts and parcels for the troops were organised and Joshua Taylor's store published a long list of winter comforts held in stock that would be welcomed by those serving at the front. These included socks, underwear, nightshirts and sleeping caps, scarves, gloves, mufflers, and flannel shirts, although family members, sewing circles (like Queen Mary's Work for Women fund, which had been established in the town shortly after the war began) or Red Cross workers would often make these garments themselves. Demand was such that more were always needed. The Cambridge Territorials were appealing for winter clothing and also for a field cooker so that they could have at least some hot food. Army kitchens were usually a fair way from the front and food often arrived cold and inedible at the trenches. Soldiers looked forward to food parcels arriving from home, which contained homemade cakes, biscuits, preserves and bottled fruits, and, hopefully, cigarettes or tobacco as well. Most at home enjoyed a decent festive dinner for this first Christmas of the war, but the same could not be said of those serving their country abroad. Nevertheless, spirits remained high and at many points along the front a Christmas Day truce was declared. Each side sang their own carols, some shouted Christmas greetings to the enemy, and in a few places, aggressors and defenders played football matches together.

Sadly such goodwill would not last.

CHAPTER 2

1915

The year began with a spate of storms that caused floods, and the River Cam burst its banks. On 8 January, the annual day of intercession was held with various church services. Recruitment initiatives continued and the local papers backed them up with lots of military news, always taking care to show the positive view. Driver H. Carter wrote home from the front:

> *I enjoyed my Christmas very well under the circumstances for we had a football match in the afternoon. We also had a camp fire in the evening, and a sing-song ... we all had a very nice present from Princess Mary and ... a photograph of the King and Queen.*

Private H.H. Robson of the 2nd Royal Scots, who had been wounded and arrived in Cambridge for treatment on Christmas Day, was awarded the VC. Mr and Mrs Lawson of Mill Road received patriotic praise for having five sons serving with the colours. The flag of the colours had been left in the university church of Great St Mary's when the Cambridge Regiment left town to go to war. The YMCA opened a new recreation hut on Cherryhinton Road for recovering wounded soldiers. A scouts' defence corps was raised at the clubroom on Newmarket Road. The military were taking over more local schools for their own occupation.

Melbourne Place School had already been requisitioned for the reserve battalion of the Cambridgeshire Regiment when it was vacated by the Cambridgeshire Battalion and the Suffolk Regiment. The university's contribution was Whewell's Court in Trinity College, which was taken to accommodate 800 men. Other schools now requisitioned included: East Road Elementary School; Eden Street School; Christchurch Institute; Milton Road infant schools; Richmond Road School; Collier Road Schools; and the Girls' County School. This meant that 700–800 children had no school, which caused huge problems. To cope with similar problems, one of the northern manufacturing towns adopted a four-tier system of education by the doubling-up of schools so that the first school had lessons with their own teachers from 9.00–10.30am and the second school had lessons with their own teachers from 10.45–12.30. In the afternoons, the first school had lessons from 1–3pm and the second school had lessons from 3–4.45pm. It wasn't an ideal situation but it did mean that all children continued to receive some education for three-and-a-half hours each day. Cambridge did not choose to adopt such a system and the education of some children was severely neglected.

Dr Sarolea, a Belgian doctor of literature from Liège, gave a talk based on his knowledge and experience gained on the battlefields of Belgium and France, in which he refuted the German allegations that the present conflict had been forced by Britain and her allies. Conditions and the unpreparedness of Britain, France and Belgium compared to the well-oiled well-prepared war machines of Germany, and Austria-Hungary was proof enough of that.

January proved to be rather a grim month. There was repeated flooding and, by the end of the month, the Cam was still flooding. Sheep's Green was under water. Newnham, Coe Fen and Chesterton Meadows were inundated and the Victoria Bridge ferry was badly affected. It was also decided that the annual boat race between Cambridge and Oxford should be abandoned for this year. Added to this was the chill of winter, rising food prices, an outbreak of scarlet fever, and further enforced reductions in street lighting and traders' lights following Zeppelin raids around the East Coast. Zeppelins flew over Cambridge as well, but the

Trinity College, Cambridge c1915

kaiser had issued explicit orders that Cambridge University was not to be bombed. A touch of humour in this grim winter was injected by a Cambridge cleric who preached robustly that: 'it was a sin to go to a wedding more joyfully than Jesus Christ went to his crucifixion and wedding feasts were the invention of the Devil.'

The war seemed to be strengthening bonds between the War Office and the Board of Agriculture and Fisheries, when a scheme of co-operation between them was inaugurated to enable local farmers' produce to be sold for the troops on more favourable terms and a promise obtained that hay would be paid for instead of being commandeered. Previously, the farmers had complained of unfair treatment by the War Office when buying or requisitioning food for men and horses. There was already a shortage of farm labour in the county due to enlistment, and this caused further problems in that farm labourers' families remained in tied cottages while their menfolk were away, which meant there was very limited accommodation for replacement workers. There were also fears that the floods would have affected the wheat harvest, although there was still an ample supply of potatoes.

At the end of January there was a meeting of the Farmers' Club at the Hotel Metropole with a lecture given on impressions of agriculture in

Australia. In that country, 600–1,000 acres were farmed singlehandedly through hard work and the use of machinery. The speaker stated that although the English produced fine crops, they worked on produce per man, not produce per acre, and he deplored English farmers' demands for higher prices and higher wages during wartime. Lessons could be learned, he said, from Australia's courage, resourcefulness and the use of machinery, and that Britain should teach men resourcefulness as well as how to earn more and produce more. However, he noted, 'custom lay heavy on them all', and there was a great resistance to change. Among British farmers there was a kind of Luddite resistance to mechanisation and also a fierce and hostile resistance to the use of alternative labour sources. Female labour was shunned, itinerant Irish labourers were not welcomed, acceptance of offers of help from boy scouts and boys in their early teens still at school was grudging. Although Cambridgeshire farmers were a little more liberal-minded than some of their northern colleagues, they were all united in their aim of trying to force the government to repatriate their sons and other experienced agricultural labourers. Every business, every industry, every service faced the same problem, that the numbers of men within a certain age range required for recruitment was causing a skills shortage. But many realised that others could be trained to do necessary work and, rather than lose out, accepted the inevitable. Women began to be employed as tram conductresses, postwomen, shop assistants, librarians, for delivering milk, and, in London, even as drivers. The suffragette movement, as soon as war broke out, had declared a truce in their often militant efforts to obtain the vote for women and vowed to give all the support they could to the country, the troops and in back-up support service. Out in the countryside, women in farming families often helped out with work on the farm, but most farmers refused to countenance any outside female help and they also refused to train any female workers.

In mid-February, the local newspaper printed a long list of those who had been recruited for Kitchener's Army, as it had become known, and King George V visited the city, inspecting the Welsh Division encamped on Parker's Piece as well as the Cambridgeshire Battalion of the Suffolk Regiment and members of B Company of the Cambridge

National Reserves. He also visited the First Eastern General Hospital and was much impressed by what he saw. In addition there were now five YMCA centres and thirty recreational centres (including one in Sidney Sussex College, another in Selwyn College and a third in Caius College) for the troops in Cambridge, providing a relaxed environment with reading, writing, games and canteen facilities. In other matters the picture was not so rosy.

At the end of February, the Cambridge Regiment suffered their first fatality when Corporal Dewey, a local man, was killed by a sniper in France. This was followed by the deaths of Captain O.N. Tebbut, who was killed in action at the front, and Lieutenant E.C. Colchester RN, who was killed on HMS *Irresistible*. A few weeks later the regiment had suffered a total of eight fatalities at the front, with twenty wounded and five missing in action.

The RSPCA had also begun to raise funds to care for sick and wounded horses. There were serious concerns that the bottled beer trade was 'to be killed by war tax', and train services were reduced both

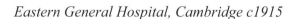

Eastern General Hospital, Cambridge c1915

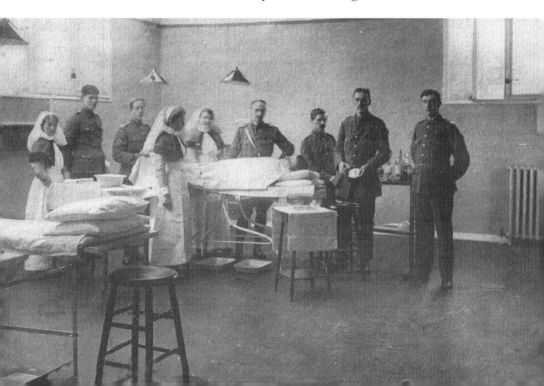

to save coal and as an economy measure. Meat and wheat prices were rising steadily. Oats were low in quality and the barley trade was 'dull'. Some bakers were also facing economic problems because families who had troops billeted with them got most of their bread from military supplies. Under DORA, all visible lights had to be either extinguished or shaded between the hours of 7pm–6am, which led to a darkening of the streets and a rise in accidents and assaults on women. Around Easter-time, a measles epidemic broke out in the city and forty-nine children died. Cheap Easter railway excursions were cancelled partly due to staff shortages but mainly because full services of goods trains were needed for collieries and munitions works, plus large numbers of trains were ordered to be kept ready for naval and military purposes.

As spring arrived there was little gaiety or frivolity and it was decided to abandon several village shows and fairs due to lack of funds and manpower, including the Histon and Impington Show and the Cambridgeshire and Isle of Ely Show, which would be hit by reduced railway services as well. There was also talk of abandoning the Cambridge Mammoth Show, where the declaration of war had first been announced the previous summer. The efforts of most people were directed towards the war and Cambridgeshire was now supporting 1,100 Belgians who urgently needed more funds for their food, clothes and accommodation. The university offered refuge to academics from Belgian universities. They had already assisted 400 Belgians but were now appealing for £1,500 (£106,500) from the Belgian Relief Fund to help with 130 professors and ninety-nine students, who were currently receiving university hospitality.

Despite dampened spirits and various difficulties, football and racing continued their normal schedules. It was generally felt that football was a good healthy sport that would keep numbers of young men fit and should be supported, while racing encouraged the keeping and care of horses. The Great War was the last war in which horses would play a part and, in 1915, there was a great need to supply horses to the front both for the cavalry and for the carriage of goods. The Cambridgeshire Hunt committee decided to carry on with the hunt as 'the extinction of this popular pack would be deplored', and whippet racing also remained

Blue Boar Hotel, Cambridge c1920

popular. Riding to hounds and dog racing perhaps showed a touch of other-world-ness, but in the countryside of Cambridgeshire and in the fens, the full effects of the war were not quite as deeply felt yet as in the towns. The Cam Sailing Club continued its activities as well (holding meetings at the Blue Boar in Trinity Street), but mainly to afford some entertainment for wounded soldiers. A political truce had been agreed for the duration of the war so no opposition was offered to the re-election of Mr Edwin Samuel Montagu, the local Liberal MP. Instead, people's attention was focused on a series of debates and discussions, talks and lectures, on all aspects of the war, and especially the role of Russia in the hostilities. The Russian fleet had met and supported other Allied fleets in the Bosphorus when the Dardanelles were closed to Allied shipping in October 1914 and had declared war on the Ottoman Empire at the beginning of November. Russia had vast manpower resources that could make a big difference to the war.

Lodging house-keepers, who had been badly hit by the war greatly reducing the numbers of university graduates and undergraduates, were facing non-negotiable rising rents from their own landlords and demands for payment of rates. Cambridge University had about 6,000 members serving with the armed forces. These included 115 'Blues' (sportsmen). Before the war there had been nearly 3,200 undergraduates. Now there were only 1,227, just over a third of the numbers a year before. Although the university billeted troops in their empty rooms, as Cambridge was deemed a military training centre, not all lodging houses were as fortunate in having paying, or at least subsidised, guests. One lodging house-keeper had earned just £11 (£787) since July 1914 and he owed £30 (£2,147). He and the other lodging house-keepers rebelled and refused to pay their rates demands. Despite being castigated by the mayor they stuck to their guns. They had no money and no income and nothing with which to pay the rates. This left the town council with a big problem of what to do about the situation. For now there seemed to be no solution.

However, there was a bigger problem facing the authorities at that time and that was the war on drink. Most Liberals wanted compulsory abstinence. This followed Lloyd George's anger at discovering that more was being spent on drink than on munitions when he addressed the question of munitions production and realised the acute shortage of shells. A white paper published at the beginning of May, based on the 'report and statistics of bad time-keeping kept in ship-building, munitions and transport areas', concluded that drinking and drunkenness were causing problems and seriously affecting output. The Master of Magdalene College proposed a motion that drastic legislation for alcohol sales should be introduced, because he said that alcohol affected men, women and munitions. Debate and argument raged from total abstention to the 'rotten concerns of breweries'. Even the king joined in the fray and issued a pledge that he had banned alcohol in royal households. The United Temperance Council of Cambridge sent a note to everyone in the town and university requesting all males and females over the age of 16 to join the national temperance movement, following the examples of King George and Lord Kitchener by taking 'the war pledge to abstain from intoxicating liquors for the duration of the war'. Fifteen thousand king's pledge papers were distributed in the borough, of which over 5,400 were returned signed and supporting the king's pledge against alcohol. The Russians had already banned sales of vodka and the French had banned sales of absinthe, while Italy taunted Britain with being a nation of morons for allowing alcohol to become a national drink and the British Navy to retain its daily ration of rum for each sailor. A kind of compromise was eventually reached when, under DORA, licensing hours were reduced from nineteen to five-and-a-half hours per day. There were howls of protest from publicans and predictions of doom, gloom and ruined businesses, but some publicans in northern towns evolved their own creative form of lateral thought. The government hadn't actually said the pubs must only open for five-and-a-half hours per day. They had simply said that alcohol could only be sold for five-and-a-half hours per day. So some northern pubs continued to open all day. They sold tea, coffee, hot Bovril and soft drinks for those going to work or taking a break. They sold soup as well at lunchtimes, and in the evening hot bedtime drinks like cocoa were sometimes added to the menu. It wasn't ideal but publicans made some income and continued to provide social meeting places for talk, companionship and games like dominoes or backgammon.

To encourage continuing recruitment, the Cambridge newspaper published a weekly roll of honour listing those who signed up to fight. A recruiting tour for town and county was organised, which went under the name of 'Follow the Drum'. Men were urgently wanted for the Suffolk Regiment. They had to be at least 5 feet 1 inch (152.5cm) in height with a 33 inch (82.5cm) chest and aged 19–38 years old, or 45 years in the case of 'old soldiers'.

A new problem was also coming to light with 'passive resisters' or 'conscientious scruplers', as conscientious objectors were called. Those in the town demonstrated their objections to war by refusing to pay rates that they believed were funding the war machine. Among those of the gown who were conscientious objectors, it became quite a fashion to put up lengthy academic and intellectual arguments, sometimes quoting obscure passages from the Bible, as to why they should be exempted from joining the armed forces and then taking their stance all the way to the appeal tribunals, where they often wasted a great deal of time. Men already serving at the front were enraged when they read accounts of these proceedings in the local newspapers that were sent out to them regularly. The arguments were diverse but the basic point of controversy was that, while conscientious objectors claimed their democratic rights to act according to their principles and conscience, soldiers and sailors had to fight in abominable conditions with great loss of life to allow them this privilege as the kaiser was not renowned for either his liberal attitudes or his concern for democracy. It was an unanswerable problem and one on which the jury is still out a hundred years later.

It was not a good time. The Cambridgeshire Regiment had sustained heavy losses and now only numbered 500 instead of the 1,000-strength that they should have had. On 22 April, the Germans introduced a new aspect to the war when they unleashed 150 tons of chlorine gas against French soldiers at Ypres, and many casualties were arriving back in Cambridge with tales of 'hell on earth' from the Western Front. In early May, even these terrible losses were overshadowed by the death of the well-known poet Rupert Brooke. Ironically, he did not die in action, although it had been his wish to do so. Brooke was a good-looking, charismatic yet deeply flawed Warwickshire poet who had won a scholarship to Kings College, Cambridge. He was a member of several distinguished poetic circles and lived for a while at the Old Vicarage in Grantchester, where he penned the well-known lines:

Stands the church clock at ten to three
and is there honey still for tea?

He was best known however for his immortal poem *The Soldier*, which begins:

If I should die,
Think only this of me:
That there's some corner of a foreign field
That is for ever England ...

Rupert Brooke with a friend at Grantchester Vicarage 1910
(courtesy of Cambridge Local Studies)

He took a commission in the Royal Naval Volunteer Reserve and, at the end of February 1915, sailed with the British Mediterranean Expeditionary Force bound for Gallipoli, but he never reached the Dardanelles. In early April he was bitten by a mosquito and fell victim to septicaemia caused by the resulting infection. Rupert Brooke died, aged 27, on 23 April (sharing the date of his death with the renowned Tudor poet and playwright William Shakespeare) in a ship moored off Skyros in the Aegean Sea, and was buried in an olive grove on the island.

There was still suspicion and hostility towards foreigners in Cambridge, especially towards those who had German-sounding names. This caused great distress as it was often only the name that had anything foreign about it. In late May, Cambridge Professor L.

Oppenheimer, who was the Whewell Professor of International Law at Trinity College, found himself needing to publicly protest his loyalty and commitment to Britain:

> *As a professor ... who ... has worked for causes of Great Britain, I think it unnecessary to give a public assurance of my loyalty to the country of my adoption ... however, in response to ... general demand, I am ready to repeat ... that Germany's attack on Belgium is the greatest international crime since Napoleon I, and that the ravaging of Belgium finds no parallel in history since the Thirty Years War ... as regards the later crimes, such as the poisoning of wells in South Africa, the use of poisonous gases, and the drowning of more than 1100 innocent men, women and children on the* Lusitania, *I cannot find words to express my feelings. These ... are not merely violations of rules of international law, but appalling outrages which have roused the righteous wrath of the world.*

RMS *Lusitania*, a modern state-of-the-art ship, was sunk by a German U-boat on 7 May 1915 off the southern coast of Ireland. Nearly 1,200 people died. The Germans were accused of breaching the International Cruiser rules, but unfortunately so had Britain. There were accusations, hotly denied, that the ship was carrying much-needed munition supplies. However, in recent years, divers have found that the ship was indeed carrying large quantities of war ammunition. Nevertheless the sinking caused a storm of protest. One hundred and twenty-eight Americans were among the dead and this was a major contributory factor to the United States joining the war on the side of the Allies two years later. Lloyd George, desperately in need of funds to redress the munitions crisis, instigated a war loans scheme in which people invested in 5s-units (about £18) for percentage returns at a later date. He called these investments 'silver bullets', since the money was to be utilised for the production of real bullets.

The prices of food, coal and gas were still rising and, as everywhere else, there were demands from many Cambridge workers for war bonuses to cope with the increasing cost of living. Potatoes and beans had suffered in unseasonal frosts. There was also a craze for white bread rather than 'the black war bread'. War bread was made from a mixture of grains and potato flour and was very dark brown in colour. Although nutritious, it was felt to be inferior. Farmers appealed for repatriation of soldiers for the harvest, rejecting the offer of help from pensioners, female labour, boy scouts and assistance from schoolboys during the school holidays. A Cambridge committee of war service for women was formed, but acceptance of female help was slow. In the town there was resistance to female tram conductresses and the Home Office shelved the idea proposed by the National Union of Women Workers for appointing female police officers. There was already an excess of females in the town, which was of greater proportion than elsewhere in the country, and also a higher proportion of older people. However, the population increased overall by 4 per cent due to the First Eastern Hospital, which had 1,470 beds and 450 staff, several hundred Belgian refugees, and the encampment of various military divisions. As the first anniversary of the war approached, arrangements were made for an intercession service in Great St Mary's, and folk took stock of how the hostilities had affected the home front in Cambridge. 'The war has led to a total upheaval of all social and business habits,' said one. Another believed that 'social barriers are fast breaking down amid the shocks of war, and ... after the war we shall never allow them to be raised again'.

Meanwhile, the Cambridgeshire Regiment was sustaining heavy losses in the Dardanelles as well as on the Western Front and large numbers of wounded soldiers from various regiments were arriving daily in the city. Over a dozen Red Cross hospitals, each with twenty to forty beds, were established, with ten around the county, the first of which was at Linton for wounded Belgian soldiers, and the remaining ones in the town. The first one to open was at St Chad's on Grange Road. This was followed by one at Cintra Terrace on Hills Road, one in Wordsworth Grove and one at Huntley on Herschel Road. Cambridge District Scouts went to Dunkirk to act as orderlies in the Red Cross hospital there and they were driving, manning and equipping Red Cross ambulances at the front. First Eastern and Addenbrookes hospital were working overtime. Addenbrookes (then still on Trumpington Street)

Linton Red Cross VAD Hospital 1915
(courtesy of Cambridge Local Studies)

was also a research hospital and its running costs for the quarter ending 15 September 1915 were nearly £1,000 (£71,000) more than for the same quarter in 1914. There were isolation hospitals at Cherryhinton and Barnwell. Fulbourn had a hospital for treating those who were mentally ill.

In 1915, the main concerns locally were infant mortality (seventy-eight deaths per 1,000 live births) and the 'white scourge' of tuberculosis or TB (seventy-three deaths in the previous year).

The Cambridgeshire and Isle of Ely Company of Royal Engineers was stationed in the town for a few days and advertised for 'shoeing and carriage smiths, blacksmiths, bricklayers, slaters, carpenters and turners, harness makers, masons, plumbers, wheelwrights and tailors to complete the establishment'. A total of forty men were needed. Just ten men volunteered. There was a route march in the town to canvass for recruits for the Cambridgeshire Regiment, but it met with only modest success. Some amusement was caused by recruiting advertisements for a bantam battalion for the 12th Suffolk Regiment. Potential recruits had to be 5ft–5ft 2 inches (150–155cm) tall with a chest measurement of 33 inches (82.5cm) when expanded. A 'khaki midsummer fair' was organised and pleas were made for munitions workers, skilled millwrights, fitters, toolmakers, turners, tool-fitters, boiler-makers, shipwrights and engineers to volunteer. Recruitment figures were causing general concern throughout the country and Lord Derby devised a scheme which, he said, would provide a national record of skills and manpower.

Towards the end of August, national registration forms under the Derby Scheme were handed out and were required to be completed by all adults. There were ten sections of information required from everyone:

1. name
2. age
3. where born
4. marital status
5. number of children
6. number of dependents
7. occupation
8. employer's name and address
9. if employed by a government department
10. work skills, adaptability and other skills.

Teachers, especially female teachers, were to help with registration scheme administration work. Many individuals and the local newspapers were suspicious that this was an attempt to gauge the number of men of military age available for call-up and that the voluntary system of enlistment was due to end. In Cambridge, although 11,000 men were already serving in the armed forces, there were still another 18,000 eligible for service. These fears turned out to be well-founded, despite initial denials. The official line was that, nationally, all men of military age would be canvassed with a view to them enlisting in sufficient voluntary numbers to avoid compulsory conscription, although Lloyd George was doubtful this ambition would be realised.

Already by the September, just thirteen months after the war started, people had begun to realise that a major aspect of education was 'about saving the state through the learning of young people'. The huge losses in manpower emphasised the need for good education so that the state could be rebuilt with the skills of a new generation. This did not equate with closing schools to provide military or hospital accommodation, but it was a question of needs must. Evening classes were provided in some subjects for older children, but some were already working part-time and, especially if they had school in the mornings, they were tired by the evening.

A Cambridge Juvenile Employment Bureau was set-up for youth work, looking after children and careers for both sexes. Girls were involved in toy-making and library work; boys had a wider choice, which included book-binding, pharmacy, the post office, motor mechanics, carpentry and a host of other occupations. Boy scouts also had the option of studying for an airman's badge. Inexplicably, the County Girls' School suspended lectures on first aid and nursing for the duration of the war. Perversely, there was much economising on school grants and education amounting to £1,209 (nearly £86,000), and scholarship grants were very limited. The Arts and Crafts School was also closed. The schools that remained open faced fuel restrictions, due to scarcity and rising prices, which meant heating was curtailed and then there was the question of the lighting orders and afternoon school hours in winter.

The Tipperary Club, for soldiers' wives and dependents, was opened in the Fitzroy Hall on Fitzroy Street. The club offered good social and material work as well as entertainment for women and their children who often lived on less than 30 shillings (£106) per week, which had to cover rent, food, fuel and clothing as a basic minimum of expenditure. A quart (1 litre) of milk now cost 5d (£1.50), eggs were six for a shilling (£1.80) and butter was 1s 7d–1s 9d (£5.10–£5.70)

King's College, Cambridge c1930

per pound (500g). Food shortages were looming as German U-boats increasingly attacked merchant shipping. There were calls for an end to improvidence and unsystematic procedures on a national basis, and for home food production, which emphasised the importance of supplies that did not have to be imported.

Potatoes, vegetables and grain were already in short supply after a disappointing harvest. Shortage of labour had made little threshing possible causing barley and oats in particular to suffer. Allotments were therefore offered at peppercorn rents and the Cambridge response was very good. As a result, considerable additions were made to permanent allotments. The university's agriculture department helped both town and county allotments and local women did good work growing crops on them, despite the fact that large numbers of farmers condemned female labour as useless. Girls were now learning horticulture and allotments provided good hands-on experience for them. In their spare time, they also collected eggs for the wounded soldiers and for military institutions.

There was a movement to make German prisoners-of-war work on the land the same as English prisoners-of-war did in Germany. Unfortunately, many farmers took patriotic zeal a little too far and refused to have the enemy working on their land, so that the military authorities had to allow furlough leave (maximum of four weeks) to soldiers from agricultural backgrounds (for which farmer's sons got preference) in order for them to help with autumn cultivation. As an alternative to manual ploughing, there was a demonstration in Cambridge of the motor plough, which would save labour. Some saw its possibilities, others regarded it with deep suspicion. It was a difficult time for agriculture but, despite everything, the wasps were having a good time of it and there were some monster nests causing real problems. A bee expert, working for Chivers (who made jams and jellies) in Histon, was finally asked to deal with them. In two months he destroyed 307 nests containing 12,000 queens and 4.5 million wasps and their grubs.

The numbers of casualties returning home was growing at an alarming rate. Within a ten-day period, 1,200 wounded men arrived from France at the Cambridge Military First Eastern hospital on West Road. Another 219 arrived a few days later, and three weeks after that, 400 more wounded men arrived over a nine-day period. Ten thousand men from Cambridge were fighting at the fronts. Of these, 470 had been killed; 700 were wounded and 300 had won distinctions and medals for bravery and gallantry in fighting. The 470 killed included 150 men from the university and a roll of honour for the fallen university men was published, prompting the retiring vice chancellor to remark that 'a creditable past causes a gloomy future'. Kings and Pembroke colleges lost considerable numbers of men and an 'inspiring memorial service' was held for them in Kings College Chapel. A big recruiting rally was held in Cambridge, with local VC and DCM heroes appealing for more enlisters, praising patriotic families like the McKays of Sawston, who had seven brothers fighting at the front. However, the record for serving members of the same family has to rest with the family of Mr and Mrs Collis, who lived on Hemingford Road in the city. Between them they had five sons, two brothers, three brothers-in-law, one son-in-law, two grandsons and fourteen nephews serving in the armed forces.

The highlight of the rally was a drumhead service on Parker's Piece and a lusty rendering of the hymn 'Fight the good fight'. Unfortunately the rally was a little overshadowed by Bronco Bill's Wild West Exhibition and Mammoth Circus on Midsummer Common, but it wasn't the real thing. Bronco Bill himself was serving a jail sentence in the United States for robbing Wells Fargo and was not released until 1917. He is not known to have visited England. The similarly named Buffalo Bill did visit England in the 1890s, and very early 1900s, but had retired in 1911. Whoever staged the show, the military authorities must have hoped that it would encourage the fighting spirit of possible enlisters.

Lord Derby's recruitment scheme was now in operation. The returned forms had been sorted into various groups such as females, males either too old or too young to fight, males in exempted occupations considered necessary for the war effort (such as agriculture, engineering, farriers, forestry, munitions, shipbuilding, etc), whose forms were 'starred', and 4,000 males of fighting age who were not in exempted occupations and whose forms had no 'star'. A copy of Lord Derby's letter explaining the situation and encouraging enlisting was sent to each of the 4,000 men. Each would then be individually canvassed by recruiting representatives, and this task was to be completed by the end of November. It was a difficult situation. The recruitment canvassers were the target of much public abuse while the local papers published letters from soldiers who had been in the trenches for months accusing non-enlisters of being 'shirkers, not doing their bit and criticising those who were'. In early November there were mysterious rumours that 'an H.G. Wellsian submarine-aeroplane-torpedo-destroyer-gunboat posing as an armoured motorboat is said to be on the way from Huntingdon to Cambridge by road'. It all sounded very *Boy's Own*, like some amazing machine of destruction with super-powers, but it turned out that a vehicle transporting a 'rather unlikely naval engineering creation' had broken down not far from Cambridge and the 'vessel' had to be left on wooden blocks on the middle of the road. Any journalistic description was, however, strictly forbidden under the terms of DORA and no one was quite certain exactly what the machine in question was. The 'boat' was launched, after several failed attempts, on the River Cam by the Pike and Eel in Chesterton, and was allegedly tested in secret at night. Eventually it was towed down to Kings Lynn and handed over to the navy.

The borough and county councils spent most of November quarrelling over road maintenance. Normally, each council maintained its own roads but major routes used equally by both were jointly maintained. The county council was trying to mend its 'deficient economic ways' with the last of its rating arrears due to be paid-up and its roads committee was always responsible for heavy expenditure. The borough council, entertaining a 'pious hope' of economy within the borough, and also mindful that it had a number of defaulting rate-payers, was trying to exact a greater road maintenance contribution from the county council, citing wartime reasons and conditions. As the conflict continued, the county council threatened to 'repudiate any payments' if the borough council allowed main roads, for which it should be responsible, to deteriorate. The borough council hit back by saying that the county council had asked for joint use of the Infectious Hospital on Mill Road, but they had refused to contribute to the maintenance of road access, and the borough council was then accused of having 'a policy of pinpricks in setting out numbers of conditions for dealing with trivial matters'.

There was also a lot of controversy over lighting in the streets. All bicycles and carts had to show a rear red light but other lighting was totally banned. DORA regulations now insisted on a complete black-out, especially as Zeppelins were active in the area. Basic provision had been made for a Zeppelin attack. There would be a hooter signal at the electric light works, even though that was likely to attract notice from the airship, distribution of fire appliances around the town, and the provision of sand in several places as well as back-up support from special constables and the Red Cross. Attack from the air was a new and disturbing development and no one really quite knew what to do for the best. Lighting restrictions were contravened many times, usually inadvertently, both by private householders and by big stores like Robert Sayle or Laurie and McConnal, and they were usually followed by prosecutions and large fines. Uniform shop closing hours of 7pm Monday–Friday and 9pm on Saturdays were suggested as one way of lessening contraventions. There were also problems with cattle-driving and signalling on roads after dark, but the most contentious issue was the use of flashlights in the streets of the town.

Darkened streets were causing all manner of problems besides a number of accidents. Street lighting was forbidden as well as shops, businesses or private houses showing lights, but Cambridge was 'asking for trouble' with the number of people using flashlights. Zeppelins could see glowing ends of cigarettes if folk smoked in the streets, or even on narrowboats on the river, so using flashlights was almost akin to marking a runway for airships. Despite numerous prosecutions, the practice continued. The borough council agreed to whiten the pavement edges for extra clarity in the darkness of the blackout, but the predilection for flashlights continued, particularly among those who belonged to the university.

Towards the end of 1915, the volunteer regiments were asked to undertake the guarding of important bridges to safeguard railway communications between coasts and garrisons. The Cambridge Volunteers were assigned to guard three bridges in and around the city. Chesterton Junction to the north was the most dangerous as it was used by large numbers of trains. Coldham's Lane Bridge was regarded as the best and a 'cushy number', because those volunteer regiment members on duty were allowed to use the nearby Borough emergency hospital as their quarters.

Probably the strangest assignment was on Lingay Fen, lying to the south of Trumpington on the south-west side of Cambridge. The fen is thought to have been mentioned by Chaucer in the Reeve's Tale. During the nineteenth century, it was renowned for 'fen skating', a sport that produced Britain's only world champion speed skater. The

Trumpington Platoon helped as well with guarding its lonely bridge, because the location was considered 'vulnerable, eerie and isolated; often dark and foggy; with muddy or frost-bound fields'.

As Christmas approached once more the town began making preparations. During the summer the Victoria Cinema had shown *The Bomb Boy* and *The Spy*, and continued the theme at Christmas with '*20,000 German Prisoners*' plus the well-read and much publicised story *High Treason*. The Playhouse offered some form of escapism with the pantomime *Aladdin*, and many watching must have dearly wished for their own genie to appear from a lamp. Local papers ran advertisements aimed at early Christmas shopping and the *Cambridge Chronicle* sponsored a weekly column for women on how to make clothes for themselves and their families. The suggestion for Christmas week gifts was a set of camisole and knickers designed in very modest fashion. War telegrams were withdrawn from the central library free reading room for reasons of economy, and there was talk of scaling down festive food in workhouses and children's homes.

The townsfolk, however, refused to let go of some of the traditional medieval merrymaking and Victorian celebration customs. The reason was that many still remembered the 'black week' of Christmas in 1899, which had been due to a number of Boer War disasters, but had been followed by 'much brighter days'. The South African campaign was regarded as 'muddled and miscalculated' and this war was seen in the same way. There had been a 10 per cent wastage of resources at government level and there was also the incalculable human cost. Many thought the present war would follow the same pattern as the Boer War and that 'much brighter days' were not far away. So town and gown made strenuous efforts to enjoy the festive season.

There were Christmas draws and lotteries held, much revelry, a Lord of Misrule, many cards, and songs and storytelling. Butchers held show nights when their Christmas provisions were dressed and displayed and carcasses were decked out with holly, ribbons and cards. Local publicans kept up the 'beef-eating' tradition and provided customers with their free annual lunch. Great rounds of cold salt beef with bread and pickles were put out and folk helped themselves.

The Red Cross held a flag day on 22 December, and in the Christmas spirit people donated 42,500 coins, which amounted to £800 (nearly £57,000). Christmas in the city was said to be 'pleasant' as people 'had become accustomed to the war'. The workhouses, St Chad's, Addenbrookes, First Eastern Hospital, children's homes and the Red Cross hospitals had a good yuletide with festive meals and entertainments and great efforts were made to ensure that everyone had a decent Christmas dinner. Cambridge workhouse, for instance, managed to provide roast beef, mutton and pork, with potatoes and parsnips, followed by Christmas pudding with a sweet sauce for its inmates. They probably fared better than the fifty lodging house-owners recently summoned to the courts for non-payment of rates.

The year ended, as it had begun, with a spate of violent weather. South-westerly gales smashed shop windows, uprooted trees and partially blew down a house. Generally, though, folk were upbeat, glad to see the back of 1915, and 'looking forward to better things' in 1916.

CHAPTER 3

1916

Intercessionary services were held on the first Sunday of the year and Cambridge entered 1916 with high hopes that this year would finally see the resolution of the war. The Cambridge newspapers praised local men and women who had 'been unprepared for war but had rallied and adapted amazingly well'. DORA lighting restrictions were having an effect and folk were shopping in the mornings rather than the afternoons. Before the war many shops remained open until well into the evening, especially on Fridays and Saturdays when several shops didn't close until 10pm or later. There were a number of contraventions of the lighting restrictions and Cambridge traders were accused of 'exposing the town to murder and mutilation' by airships. Some London stores now encouraged an early morning shopping trend by offering 'shopping breakfasts' and it was hoped that Cambridge stores might follow suit.

In the county concerns were voiced about the dangers of shepherds and drovers driving their flocks and herds along darkened roads, but there seemed to be few accidents. Drinking had also decreased as a result of the DORA licensing restrictions and the local Star Brewery lamented much-reduced sales owing to the heavy duty on beer, although sales of spirits generally had increased.

All forms of public gambling, gaming or betting, including slot machines, were now illegal, to enable folk to put their money to better use. Following the Naval and Military Pensions Act of 1915, the county council had set-up a local war pensions committee for administration purposes. The borough MP, Almeric Paget, gave £2,000 (£121,100) to the city's relief fund for distress caused by the war. The county and borough councils, bickering like an old married couple, were not co-operating well. The county council was successfully resisting borough efforts and dragging its heels over equipping the Arts and Crafts School for classes on munition production and as a munitions works on the grounds that training and equipping would take time and money and the war might be over before completion. The borough council was pre-occupied by controversy with Chesterton RDC, who believed that they had not received adequate financial recompense following an extension of the borough that occupied Chesterton RDC land. The borough council claimed they had only paid half the agreed amount because they had taken over the sewage departments of Cherryhinton and Grantchester as well, and had also relieved those places of the remaining portions of debt incurred by managing their own sewage departments. Both councils insisted that the other had gone back on their word. Chesterton RDC was particularly aggrieved because they were also providing for the mentally ill in the local asylum as well as their road maintenance expenditure contribution, while the borough and county councils were still quarrelling over who should pay what for road maintenance. Meanwhile, Mitchams Stores of Chesterton decided to briefly forget that there was a war on and held a two day sale of high class furs.

Khaki armlets had been introduced and were worn by those on leave, those in exempted occupations and those either discharged from the forces or medically unfit to serve, to avoid the cruel and often unjustified taunts of cowardice dished out by the White Feather Brigade. This was an organisation of mostly young females who had taken it upon themselves to vilify any man not wearing uniform without first ascertaining the reason and presenting them with a white chicken feather as a symbol of their perceived cowardice. Although recruitment was steady, there was still great controversy caused by married men with families enlisting while young single men held back and often stepped into well-paid recently vacated jobs. Cambridgeshire and the Isle of Ely Territorial Forces Association had spent 1915 bringing different county units up to strength and raising a company of Royal Engineers. In addition, the 3rd/1st and 4th/1st Cambridgeshire regiments and the 13th Battalion Suffolk Regiment (Cambridgeshire) took part in appealing to attesters to join the county regiments. The war had also greatly decreased the number of prisoners as they joined up and Cambridge county gaol on Castle Hill was closed on grounds of economy. However, as Lloyd George had feared, voluntary enlistment under the Derby Scheme of 1915 was not producing sufficient numbers of men to replace the huge numbers being lost, killed and wounded, and the prime minister, H.H. Asquith, introduced the Military Service Bill in early January. It received the Royal Assent on 27 January and became a lawful Act on 2 March.

Under the conditions of the Military Service Act, all men aged 18–41 years of age could be called-up for army service unless they were married, a widower with children, serving in the Royal Navy, a minister of religion, or working in a reserved occupation of benefit to war service. This naturally evoked howls of outrage from single men and a second Act in May 1916 extended compulsory call-up for military service to married men as well. Objections to call-up would be heard by military services tribunals, who had the powers to grant conditional or temporary exemption. There was also a right of appeal to County Appeals Tribunals. Four main grounds for exemption now included:

- men already engaged in war work or training for work beneficial to the war
- serious hardship would ensue in exceptional financial or business or domestic situations
- ill health or infirmity
- conscientious objectors

It was the last category that caused the most controversy, ill feeling and hardship. It was argued that Britain was a free country and men should have the right to follow their principles and their consciences. This was not in dispute, but unfortunately the kaiser was not noted for his democratic or liberal views and if the kaiser conquered Britain no one would have any right to follow any individual principles. The right of the state was fundamental in German thinking and education. Therefore, the kaiser had to be resisted in order to protect Britain's democratic rights and freedoms and someone had to fight him. It was an insoluble dilemma. Many conscientious objectors compromised and volunteered for the medical services or non-combatant duties. Those who refused any compromise were either imprisoned or went on the run. They were generally reviled and scorned and life could be extremely difficult and unpleasant for them. Many lived rough and stole food from outlying farms. Anyone who knowingly helped a conscientious objector could also be imprisoned. There was a huge social stigma as well, which would continue long after the war had ended when known conscientious objectors were deprived of the right to vote for several years.

The economic teeth of the war were now beginning to cause some pain. Free trade principles were being subsumed as tariffs and taxes became necessary both for regulation and to raise extra income. The Cambridge Bill Posting Company was losing business steadily as a direct result of the war. There was to be no pleasure boating at all on the Cam this year, and local keepers suspended all but the most essential work on the river for the sake of economy. The county council had labour problems caused by staff enlisting, which led to further economies in road maintenance. The council had also issued warrants to the Overseers of the Poor in twenty-two of its parishes for rates arrears. The idea was to levy rates by distress and the sale of goods. Farmers and market gardeners were urged to increase production of food, but most male agricultural workers were being taken for military service. The 'gigantic muddle' caused by the starring of certain agricultural occupations under Lord Derby's scheme led many of the public to believe farmers and their sons had tried to evade military service, and there was a general lack of sympathy for agriculture and its workers. In addition, agriculture in particular was not only slow to consider the idea of female labour but was often actively hostile.

It was generally thought that female labour was an untrained waste of time. Few farmers were prepared to train women, fewer would accept female labour on their farms. However, it was rapidly becoming Hobson's choice.

The actual expression 'Hobson's choice' originated from Thomas Hobson (1544–1631), who was a Cambridge carrier. He rented out horses from his stables near St Catherine's College. The fastest horses were always the most popular and became overworked. Therefore, Hobson evolved a system and established a strict rotation of the animals whereby those renting an animal could only take the next in line, which was usually tethered by the stable doors. Those who refused didn't get to rent a horse, so Hobson's choice became not so much a question of choice but a take-it-or-leave-it policy. The choice was something or nothing.

The government was becoming heartily fed up with the need to repatriate farmer's sons at harvest or ploughing-time and the need for women land workers was becoming paramount. The National Union of Women Workers was enthusiastic and keen to promote the idea. 'The training and work of women on the land is one of the most remarkable results of the war affecting the labour market', and the Woman's Farm and Garden Union was initiated to help those working on the land. The University Agricultural Department helped the War Agricultural Committee to train women for land and farming work. Food shortages were looming mainly due to:

- improvidence in using available supplies
- unsystematic procedures in distribution
- German submarine campaign against British merchant shipping

There were already shortages of potatoes and vegetables and local allotments were offered at peppercorn rents to encourage a grow-your-own policy. The response in Cambridge was so good that considerable additions were made to permanent allotments and the University Agricultural Department helped with the county allotments as well. Women were doing sterling work. Many women, country women, farmers' wives and those who grew their own, either in a small garden or on an allotment, already knew the basics of good horticultural husbandry.

One lady in Dorset, with just the help of her two small boys, had produced from her allotment:

- 60 bundles of asparagus
- 50 bundles of rhubarb
- 80 pounds of tomatoes
- 600 lettuces
- 10 bushels of spinach
- 20 bushels of onions
- 2 hundredweight of carrots
- 2 hundredweight of parsnips
- 3 bushels of artichokes
- 120 pounds of peas
- 210 pounds of runner beans
- 2 sacks of broad beans
- 10 bushels of beetroot
- 210 vegetable marrows
- 30 cucumbers
- 3.5 tons of potatoes.

Pleased by the general female response, the government announced its intention to raise an 'army' of 400,000 women to work the land, in uniform and for a proper wage, not as sweated labour. It was intended that they should also work at fruit-picking, butter and cheese-making, feeding stock, rearing calves, looking after pigs and poultry, as well as hoeing, weeding, haymaking, manure spreading, planting and picking potatoes, and any other jobs required on the farms. Many farmers were totally resistant to the idea, digging in their heels in intransigent and short-sighted ways. Women might be willing, they said, but were they fit to be out in all weathers and roughing it like farm labourers, ignoring the fact that many country women already did just that? There were questions over rising at 4am to milk cows, although English milkmaids had traditionally done so in past centuries. Women were not deemed capable of bagging up cabbage greens on frosty mornings, clearing out pigsties or spreading manure. Besides, argued the farmers, women have children to look after, meals to cook, homes to run. How could they possibly manage everything? Some might not be physically fit. They sneered at the upper-class women who considered themselves physically fit. The whole thing, said the farmers, might look good on paper but begged the question of who is going to do the hardest and most unpleasant duties and for what pay? Agricultural work was always low-paid and, besides, farm labourers' wives with six children didn't need any lessons in home economics.

The government promised to examine the rates of low pay, especially for the hardest work. But the farmers remained inflexible, despite one 72-year-old lady from the county who insisted that she could 'plough very well', as well as any man.

The government was fast losing patience and some members voiced the opinion that many farmers were simply selfish and wanted their sons back. Didn't everyone? However, the farmers' general responses to the idea of female labour simply hardened the government's resolve that trained and organised female labour was to be offered and those who didn't accept it would simply go without manual help.

Increasing numbers of wounded soldiers continued to arrive in Cambridge. There were extensions and alterations to Addenbrookes' Hospital. First Eastern General Hospital made 100 beds available to the War Office. Military hospitals like First Eastern, large sprawling complexes of single-storey huts in grid formation, were built in a number of places, emphasising a huge need and the sheer number of wounded soldiers requiring medical treatment. VAD Red Cross hospitals, like those at Cintra House on Hills Road and at Whittlesford, Swavesey, Linton, Histon, Impington and a number of other places gave what extra help they could. By March there was some controversy over responsibility for sanctioning and maintaining military hospitals but there was an even bigger concern which was causing much tension.

A number of soldiers coming to Cambridge for medical treatment were bringing sexually transmitted diseases (STDs) with them, chiefly syphilis. The newspapers described the local 'panic' that had resulted and the insistence upon treatment of these soldiers at local isolation hospitals like Cherryhinton and Barnwell. Many had ignored Kitchener's pleas to behave with restraint, courtesy and total morality while on active service abroad, but with war conditions as they were it was difficult to blame those who had strayed. Military commanders, of course, were quick to blame the women, saying that 'innocent soldiers were being led astray by dissolute women'. The main problem was that those being treated for STDs had often recovered from their wounds and were restless. The fear was that if they went out from the hospitals for some recreation they would become friendly with local girls and, in some cases, spread their STDs further. This fear was not without foundation and there were several heated exchanges on the subject with some suggesting that Cherryhinton and Barnwell hospitals should be fenced and guarded like proper prisons and that inmates should not be allowed out until they had made a full recovery. Treatment for syphilis was pretty horrendous, involving arsenic-based injections and the use of mercury-based creams. The poisonous properties of such treatments were not realised at the time and may ultimately have done as much or more damage (they could cause skin cancer) than the disease itself.

Another growing infection, just as serious, if not more so, that the medical authorities were trying cope with as well was TB, which was still robbing many thousands of young people of their lives every year. Tuberculosis is airborne and therefore patients needed to be isolated. Cambridge University had done a great deal of research into TB, its causes and treatment, and in 1915, Dr Pendrill Varrier-Jones was appointed as TB officer for Cambridgeshire. Based on this research and his observations, he concluded that a good diet and plenty of fresh air, as well as medical treatments, were essential for the welfare of TB patients, and in 1916 he established the Cambridgeshire Tuberculosis Colony in the Cambridgeshire village of Bourn. Part of the treatment included open-sided bedrooms on the same principle as open-sided wards, used at First Great Eastern Hospital in the town. Patients were given financial support and encouraged to work as part of their rehabilitation. He had visions of a self-supporting community that would care for its inmates like an extended family during their convalescence, a similar concept to the leper colony off Crete so vividly imagined and described by Victoria Hislop in her book *The Island* published ninety years later. In 1918, the TB colony moved to Papworth Hall, which today houses the acclaimed Papworth Heart Hospital where the first pacemaker procedures and the first heart transplant operations were carried out in the latter half of the twentieth century.

The Royal Society for Arts was now holding examination in English for Belgian refugees and other foreigners in Cambridge. The Belgians were incredibly grateful for all the townspeople were doing and to the university for offering its full academic facilities. Many Belgians took local hospitality only for as long as they needed to establish themselves and to learn a good basic standard of English. In Cambridge, the Hügel Homes scheme for Belgian families had been initiated by Baroness Anatole van Hügel, who believed that it was difficult and unkind to break up family groups. The Belgian ladies helped the war effort with sewing parties and packing up parcels for the Belgian comforts fund, or by visiting Belgian soldiers in the First Eastern Hospital. The refugees, however, were steadily moving on and only twenty-nine were now left in the Hügel Homes.

The economic screws continued to turn, meanwhile. Food and fuel prices were still rising steadily and milk-watering-down frauds were becoming very common. Wheat prices were now 54s.6d (approximately £166) a quarter and barley was scarce. Hot cross buns as an Easter treat were discontinued for the second year running. Pears soap was selling itself on the basis that it had been the preferred soap of Wellington and that it was the soap of choice for war orders. The soap was preferred because it didn't soften through use and lasted better, so it was more economical. There were more postal restrictions with only two deliveries a day, at 7am and 11.15am, and no afternoon or evening deliveries. Additional taxes had been levied on sugar, cocoa and mineral waters, as well as amusements and entertainments, while new taxes had been put on railway tickets and matches. The borough and county councils had been ordered to make savings on an annual basis.

The university had its own council, which made very generous donations to war causes in the town, county and nationally. The borough council managed to make a saving of £6,600 (nearly £400,000) from paving and lighting, although most of the savings came from lighting due to the DORA restrictions, and a smaller amount from public health. This gave the borough a proposed reduction of 6d (£1.50) in the rates. The county economised on general purposes and higher education while increasing expenditure for certain special purposes and elementary education, which resulted in a proposed 4.5d (£1.12) saving. Colonel T.W. Harding had produced a paper on agriculture stating that pre-war imported wheat had been cheaper, so that 3,000,000 acres went out of cultivation from arable to pastoral 1881–1911 and there had been no growth in the agricultural industry for years. This was the reason for poor production and low wages. Land was now bought for prestige, esteem and acclaim, not for working, so that owning land was a luxury the poor man could not afford. He concluded that it was essential that agriculture become a paying business once more.

In April, an auction was held to raise funds for the agricultural relief of those in Allied countries and a cockerel was sold for a record £1,035 (just over £74,000). Despite hardships, Cambridge folk still supported local flag days and fundraising for the troops, although there were concerns that the Easter uprising in Dublin might affect the Irish flag day due to be held on 13 May. In the event, the 'Wearing of the Green' flag day raised £145.14s.6d (just over £9,000), showing there was still considerable sympathy for the Irish who wanted separation from Westminster, but reflecting perhaps some hesitation since the flag day held by the YMCA just three days earlier towards funding a YMCA hut in France raised £325 (nearly £20,000).

There had been severe floods in early May. Some villages and 20,000 acres were under water between Littleport and Downham Market. By mid-May, however, 'there was much green foliage, lilac and laburnham [sic] blooms bursting out'. Histon and Impington Boys Brigade were actively assisting war work with collections of waste paper and had collected two tons for the War Services Committee. The Scouts kept on top form for home defence and war defence, and the newspapers continued to praise patriotic families who had a number of members serving in the forces. Mr and Mrs Worland of Cottenham had five sons in the army and the Peaching family of Bottisham had five sons and a grandson serving, while Mr and Mrs Lowings of Cambridge had eight sons and two sons-in-law at the front. Military weddings increased as soldiers and their sweethearts took their chance at happiness while there was still time. Pretty military weddings, like that between Lieutenant Charles Stubbs and Miss Lucy Lavender, which took place in early May, were reported weekly.

Weddings in 1916 were less lavish than today. Brides with more money might wear a white dress and have a proper sit-down wedding breakfast, but for many it was very low-key. Female relatives often made the dress, which was a smart 'Sunday best' affair that could be worn on many future occasions, and a small wedding cake. After the ceremony there would just be cups of tea and a piece of cake for the guests. There was usually neither time nor money for a honeymoon. Patriotism and news of weddings were upbeat but elsewhere the story was mixed.

Tribunals had begun hearing appeals against compulsory call-up. The county council was criticised for setting a bad example by requesting exemption for their town clerk and their dentist. The dentist possibly was in an essential post, but the town clerk's duties could be done by someone else, even a woman, and there were grumbles that 'women were claiming the right to intrude themselves everywhere'. Many were outraged by a visit of Sylvia Pankhurst to Cambridge, and she was accused of being adopted by the university as a symbol for conscientious objectors. The county council declared itself unwilling to employ conscientious objectors, and so did many other employers. The tribunals took a firm line over conscientious objection. It could not be supported by concrete evidence and conscientious objectors risked being sent to gaol if they did not agree to work for the war effort in some capacity. Four types of war work were usually offered:

- VTC (voluntary training corps)
- VAD (voluntary aid detachments like the Red Cross)
- fire brigade
- special constables.

One conscientious objector, a Quaker socialist, who was actually working with the Friends' ambulance unit in France, had returned to protest about compulsory conscription. Another objector was a Christadelphian, who stated that his religion would allow him to make munitions but not to fight. The university was also giving the impression that it was against compulsory conscription. There were numbers of students and professors claiming exemptions, and those in the field of economics seemed to be especially pro-pacifism. One university student said that invasion by the Germans was not the worst evil, while another university student felt that he would not be able to take Holy Orders if he went to war. However, one enterprising and educated member of the Cambridge tribunal quoted the Book of Numbers xxxii, verses 5–7 and 20–28 in which Moses advocates war on enemies:

Shall your brethren go to war, and shall ye sit here? If ye will go armed before the Lord to war until He hath driven out His enemies ... ye shall return ... guiltless before the Lord ... but if ye will not do this ... ye have sinned against the Lord.

Over fifty appeals for exemption from military service were heard, but most grounds concerned possible hardships and single men were at pains to point out that they had responsibilities and dependants just the same as married men. Many appeals were dismissed. Although Tripos numbers were well down (thirty-seven for Natural Sciences instead of the usual 170, and seven for Classics instead of 100), the university had pleaded for several academic posts in order to maintain the teaching and output. Some university and exam board posts were declared exempt or given a temporary or time-limited exemption but, again, most appeals were dismissed. There were a number of exemption categories for agricultural workers so that they did not need to go before the tribunals. The farmers were not giving up.

They still wanted soldiers for the harvest. Squads of soldiers were offered from First Eastern Hospital and the two military hospitals at Cherryhinton and Barnwell. As the last two hospitals were treating those with STDs, the farmers refused, but there seemed little reason to refuse those from First Eastern. The farmers insisted that there should be more liaison between the Department of Agriculture and the War Office, but what they meant was that they wanted their sons repatriated. No one else it seemed would do, least of all women. The farmers continued to insist that female workers were unwilling to go with the horses but the men were used to them. They also obtained fairly generous exemptions for farm hands.

Ploughmen/horsemen
- light land – one man up to 60 acres
- arable land – one man up to 240 acres
- extra 75 acres and above – one extra man

Cowmen
- one man and assistance from women and boys for every 15 cows in milk

Shepherds
- one man to every 20 sheep not including lambs

Stockmen
- one man to every 40 head of store stock

Stacker/Thatcher
- one man to every 100 acres under hay; and corn crops if other thatchers employed

However, there were still complaints about labour shortages caused by recruitment. Indeed, the Cambridgeshire War Agricultural Committee talked of little else. Farmers were also complaining about feeding their own animals on hay, preferring to sell it to the military but waiting until the cost was right. After the Paris conference of the Allies on war strategies and trade after the war, Lloyd George had remarked that the obsession with this war seemed to be money. His supposition was confirmed when Andrew Bonar Law announced that the Paris conference would safeguard trade after the war and that 'markets and profits won't

Trinity College gateway c1872

be stolen away', while a high-ranking businessman insisted that Britain 'wasn't yet ready to win the war'. Around the same time a Cambridge tribunal allowed rates collectors and rates clerks exemption from military service. The obsession with profit found ultimate expression when the residents of Tenison Road, Lyndewode Road and St Barnabas Road decided on a bit of self-help, and a cabbage patch was begun in the public garden at the junction of the three roads. It was noted, doubtless by someone from the rates department, that this venture should 'attract the ratepayers' attentions as there might be possible profits involved'.

Finally the farmers got their way and four weeks' furlough was granted to soldiers from the regular and territorial forces for the harvest season. Pay was to be at the rate of 5/- (£15) per ten-hour day exclusive of two hours allowed for meal breaks. Many members of the government were furious at the expense, inconvenience and downright impracticalities forced on them by the stubborn intransigence of the farmers, and it was determined that this would be the very last time. If the war was still continuing in the summer of 1917, then the farmers would be given no choice. They would use the labour of female workers, scouts, schoolboys on holiday, or, possibly, German prisoners-of-war, or they would go without manual assistance at harvest-time.

On 21 May, Daylight Saving Time, or what is now known as British Summer Time (BST), came into operation for the first time. It was the brainchild of William Willett, who thought that so many early morning hours of daylight were being wasted during the summer and that it would save on the cost of lighting. Most people accepted the idea, although there were a few grumbles, chief among them the farmers, and the Farmers' Union vigorously opposed the Daylight Saving Act. They had mistakenly assumed that, with the clocks going forward by one hour, those who did the milking would have to get up at 3am as the 4am of BST was really 3am, having completely failed to recognise the fact that absolutely everything was moved on for one hour during the summer.

In the first week of June, the whole country was shocked to learn of the death of Lord Kitchener. His ship, HMS *Hampshire*, hit a mine to the west of Orkney and sank rapidly. Lord Kitchener drowned and a memorial service was held for him in Great St Mary's Church. General Sir Douglas Haig took over Kitchener's command on the eve of what was to become one of the most infamous battles in history.

The people of Cambridge were beginning to feel that, despite the summer, there really wasn't much to which they could look forward. The war was dragging on seemingly without end and casualties were growing. Food and fuel were becoming ever more expensive. Much milk was either deficient in milk fats or watered down. Pleasure boating on the Cam was forbidden. The town's open spaces and parks were in poor shape after use as army encampments, and Romsey Cricket Club members volunteered to work on the restoration of Parker's Piece so that they could play cricket there during the summer. A lot of the ceremonial surrounding the Midsummer Fair was suspended.

The university abandoned May Week along with the balls, boat races, champagne, sports, concerts and theatre that were attendant upon it. The only exception seemed to be a land and water gymkhana held for army cadets on Trinity College lawns.

War savings certificates were issued for a war savings week in mid-July. Each certificate cost 15s 6d (£46.50), but they would be worth £1 (£60) in five years' time and no individual would be allowed to hold more than 500 certificates. Female labour was becoming grudgingly accepted, even in grocers' shops, but they were not allowed to cut up any of the provisions. Women were training to be clerks, shop assistants, postwomen and bus conductresses, and they were also learning how to work on the land. Their traditional chores of cleaning, cooking, washing, ironing and sewing were not neglected but had become of more secondary importance to the war effort.

There were complaints, however, that local children looked dirtier than before the war and that this was due to laxness on the part of single mothers in the absence of fathers who would have kept a stricter eye on the children. Often it was a question of priorities. Was it more important to make a contribution to the war effort and to put food on the table, or was it more important to constantly ensure a child's face was scrubbed clean? It was just another sacrifice for the war.

The Germans were conducting a U-boat campaign against all British merchant shipping, the idea being to sink as many as possible and hopefully starve Britain into submission. Foodstuffs were becoming more expensive and there were beginning to be shortages in supplies. Urgent talks were held with the local farmers to discuss the deficiencies in home-grown supplies. 60 per cent of meat was being produced from the country's own resources, but only 25 per cent of butter, 20 per cent of bread and cheese, and there were no official figures for eggs. Meat supplies were also vulnerable to the costs of animal feeding stuffs like maize, linseed and cotton cakes. If more pasture land was turned over to arable use, this would have a knock-on effect on livestock. But it was becoming imperative to increase grain crops, especially wheat. However, like lots of places in the country, Cambridge was slow to adapt to the idea of managing and conserving food consumption.

The idea of a hearty breakfast, which included bacon and eggs or chops and slices of cake with tea, followed by luncheons and dinners, particularly within the academic and hospital environments, was still prevalent. Compared with many towns and cities, particularly in the north of England, Cambridge was a quite a wealthy town. The lodging house-keepers were having a very hard time but, again unlike their northern counterparts, the town's industries and businesses were not, as yet, suffering unduly. In many northern mill-towns breakfast was simply porridge, dinner (eaten at midday) was meat and two vegetables, or potato pie for the poorer folk, with a slice of bread and jam for tea. Cheap wartime recipes were published and a dark barley war bread was advocated. Hoarding and profiteering were rife in Cambridge, as everywhere else, despite constant government pleas for folk to buy just what they needed with no extra, and for better-off shoppers to buy more expensive cuts of meat, leaving the cheaper cuts for the poor. Sugar was becoming a problem. Nationally, everyone seemed to prefer white sugar in carefully formed lumps. Granulated sugar was mostly regarded with disdain, as was brown sugar, except for cooking. There was a move to grow sugar beet and process it within Britain and this was gaining momentum, but it still did not have government support. The farmers were still pleading acute general labour shortages so vagrants were put to work on the land in both town and county, which the local Poor Law Guardians said was a failure, and pensioners were allowed to be employed without losing their very meagre pensions, generally 5/- (£15) per week.

To the alarm of many, the inmates of Fulbourn and Chesterton asylums, for those with mental health problems, were allowed to cut hay with scythes, although some labour on the land by female patients seems to have been acceptable. Farmers were now discussing how agriculture would be after the war, slowly beginning to recognise the advance of mechanisation and that post-war prices would never return to their pre-war levels.

Nearly 11,000 men from the town and county were now serving in the armed forces and another 7,000 were eligible for call-up. The absence of breadwinners was having an increasing effect. Cambridgeshire and the Isle of Ely Soldiers and Sailors Families Association had now offered or given relief in 5,515 cases. There was growing concern over the welfare of local prisoners-of-war who, it was feared, would starve without the regular food parcels sent from the town. Cambridge men serving with the forces were suffering heavy casualties. Four hundred wounded soldiers arrived for treatment in only two days. Shortly afterwards, the one hundredth ambulance train drew in to Cambridge Railway Station. Finally, news filtered through from the Somme, 'the great battle raging on the Western Front'.

Haig, confident the battle would last just one day and end in German defeat, had brought in the new-fangled movie cameras to record the event that began on 1 July and was still raging in mid-November. The battle was a major turning point in the First World War. Until then folk had seen the war as glorious and honourable. Now they saw it as bloody, messy and wasteful and these views were reflected in the verse of the war poets. Cynicism had crept in and, while it did not lessen the war effort, many people lost faith in both the generals and the government.

Troops at Cambridge station c1916

At the Fitzroy Hall in Wellington Street, the Tipperary Club unveiled a roll of honour for relatives of its members. Lord French came to the town for an inspection of troops on Parker's Piece and paid tribute to the Cambridgeshire Regiment. Some families, like the Hobbs of Cambridge, had several members of their family wounded during a very short time. Local hospitals struggled to cope. New wards were built at First Eastern Hospital. Addenbrookes was causing anxiety as costs and cash-flow were hampering the alteration of old buildings and the changes were causing a depletion of staff. Addenbrookes, like Ashton General Hospital in Lancashire, was doing valuable and pioneering work with X-rays. Cambridge Nursing Association, looking to the future, had realised that maternity and child welfare were of paramount importance in replacing the generation that was being lost on the battlefields. Midwifery skills were essential and so too was 'clean milk' together with improvements in hygiene. One hundred and fifty Serbian boys, rescued when Serbia collapsed under the toll the war had taken, had arrived as refugees in Cambridge, many not knowing if their parents and families were still alive or not. Throughout August, there were more heavy casualties on the Western Front, 'the trenches choked with the dead'. As if this wasn't enough, the Home Front was coping with an outbreak of swine fever and in the middle of it all the working of the Cambridge Corporation sewage farm completely broke down and the River Cam was polluted with raw sewage.

Intercession services were held in Cambridge as the war entered its third year, but the spirits of many in town, gown and county were low. August bank holiday was ignored and treated as just another working day. Cambridge scout troops collected newspapers and helped with cleaning up the river and harvesting. VTCs, schoolmasters and prisoners-of-war were also available to help with harvesting, and county farmers were criticised for lack of consideration when they insisted on having soldiers and their sons returned from the front to help as well. No one bothered much with taking holidays and those who did crowd the pleasure resorts were heavily criticised. Some workers received war bonuses to help with the high cost of living, while some did not receive any extra money, and this caused resentment and controversy.

Cambridge Corporation had been paying those employees who enlisted war allowances, but not those men called-up under the compulsory Military Services Act. Those of their wives who had no children were now paid reduced amounts and told to get a job. Alcohol was banned for all military personnel in Cambridge on the grounds that it could hinder recovery and, anyway, drunken troops would be of no use. There was an outcry because no cake or jam was included in the Fulbourn Asylum dietary, followed by another outcry that local dentists were being called-up.

Cambridge Workhouse authorities, trying to practise a little self-sufficiency, were disappointed when denied permission to keep hens in their gardens. Cambridge Suffrage Association met at Newnham to discuss women and the vote. They declared that the self-sacrificing work women were doing as part of the war effort deserved voting inclusion in the new Registration Bill, which was being debated, and that in the interests of labour, social reform and domestic government, women should not be left out of the franchise. There was a great deal of support for this view, not least from the government, but there was still a lobby who believed that women 'should not worry their pretty little heads with vile politics', and that 'women have not the brain power to cope with running a home, bringing up children and deciding which way they should vote'. One anti-suffragette campaigner actually brought it down to the economics of drawing up a new register, citing that as a reason for not giving women the vote. Another writer 'felt it to be our duty to resist the indiscriminate granting of the franchise to every man without regard to fitness and qualification … neither manhood suffrage nor woman suffrage ought to be conceded in the middle of a great war … the great principles for which we have fought so long may be sacrificed to radical clamour'.

The gown had already devoted many resources and much research to the war effort, particularly in the fields of agriculture, science and engineering, and a university PhD holder pleaded the importance of scientific work and the organising of examinations as grounds for exemption from military service. The engineering department labs in Free School Lane had been presented with a captured German Albatross plane in recognition of their scientific services rendered in the war. The university announced that the plane would go on public show and proceeds would be donated to the British Red Cross Society.

The Master of Emmanuel College claimed exemption for an employee in the university library who dealt with periodicals and binding, on the grounds that periodicals should still be obtained from Germany under a special Board of Trade permit for importation, and a three-month temporary exemption was granted. The record, however, of successful claims for exemption from military service belonged to employees of Chivers in the Cambridgeshire village of Histon. Chivers were mostly well-known for their jams and jellies. The company put in over a hundred claims for their married employees and all but one (who had no children) were allowed. Generally, men over the age of 30 were granted conditional exemptions while men under the age of 30 were granted temporary exemptions. Some agricultural workers abused their exemptions granted by Chesterton Military Tribunal by leaving the farms on which they were working and taking up beating for shooting parties.

The government requested the newly opened Victoria Cinema on Market Hill to show the film *For the Empire*. The cinema followed this with 'the world's greatest film', namely *Battle of the Somme*, which was also shown by the Playhouse on Mill Road. King George V, Queen Mary and Queen Alexandra had already seen the film and the king encouraged his subjects to follow suit, saying 'the public should see these pictures that they may have some idea of what war means'. It was said that the guns of Flanders could be heard in Cambridge and most of the public already knew what the war meant, perhaps even more personally than the king, but they went because they wanted to know exactly what their loved ones were facing. Many were utterly horrified and the cinemas had to give first aid to those for whom it was just too much. It might have been a similar reaction that prompted the local newspaper to voice its upset that some women were braiding their hair in German fashion, condemning this as 'part of the insinuating way in which German ideas are spread among the people of this country'. The paper completely ignored the fact that braiding hair was simply a safe

Trinity College in snow c1906

and practical way of keeping long hair out of machinery, out of food and generally out of the way.

There was a great variety of occupations currently on offer for girls and this resulted in a huge drop in applications for domestic work, which was hard, unremitting and poorly paid. Chesterton RDC had even been so bold as to hire a female shepherd. While the scouts practised methods of attack and defence in exercises on the east side of Cambridge, army recruitment was proving, perhaps unsurprisingly, to be 'disappointingly slow'. Despite the patriotic records of women like Mrs Kidman of Girton who had six sons in the army and Mrs Cundell of Cottenham who had seven sons serving in the forces, few were anxious, in the wake of the Somme, to actively put themselves forward. The army clothing scandal of late September did nothing to reassure people that those who enlisted were seen as much more than dispensable cannon fodder. A network conspiracy of dishonesty, fraud and blackmail had been discovered in the Royal Army Clothing Department, which made it virtually impossible for honest contractors manufacturing decent clothing and boots to sell their wares to the army without paying large commissions and exposing themselves to blackmail. Coupled with the 'shells scandal' of 1915, when inefficient dithering caused a severe shortage of explosive shells and left troops defenceless in the trenches, plus the general disorganised inability to provide troops with adequate rations or shelter, not to mention the low and sporadic army pay, there was little to persuade the ordinary man that the authorities cared one jot about personal welfare or properly equipping men to fight battles. There were too many horror stories about conditions in the trenches, the cold, the hunger, the deprivations, and the effects of chlorine gas, to encourage men to volunteer. Furthermore, free medical treatment for the dependants of soldiers and sailors had ceased at the end of August.

Despite the promise of 'a land fit for heroes for those who returned, many discovered that this mythical land did not exist. Others were now doing the jobs they had left when they enlisted and there were few opportunities or resources for those maimed or blinded by the war. The Cambridge War Pensions Committee was agonisingly slow to do much at all and this caused severe hardship in many cases. The idea of settling ex-servicemen on the land was both a fascinating and a disappointing scheme, largely doomed by the farmers' reluctance to release tied cottages, which they wanted for their own labourers. The state had a duty to build reasonably decent and affordable homes for discharged servicemen, but no money or materials with which to do so as long as the war continued.

Cambridge University faced a grim new academic year and freshers got what was described as a damp welcome. There were only 156 of them (the Michaelmas term of 1913 had taken on 3,263 undergraduates), making a total of just 444 students, seven eighths below the normal tally, and the whole future of the university was now in question. For the first time since the medieval origins of the university there were proposals for new degrees and post-graduate work to be initiated plus lengthening of terms, revision of courses, and simplification of exams and Tripos, much to the annoyance of traditionalists, particularly one measure the university proposed to adopt, which was that Greek should be made optional instead of compulsory for Cambridge entrance. It was also decided that the English Tripos should be adapted and separated from medieval and modern languages. English would be divided into one unit on medieval and modern literature and one unit on early literature and history.

A Cambridge councillor attacked the British system of elementary education as a failure, urging the adoption of the metric system, which would save valuable time and prove a great gain in the teaching of mathematics. But his pleas fell on deaf ears. The low number of students was a blow to local industries that largely depended on undergraduates, especially the lodging house-keepers, although some of these were now taking billeted troops. However, there were local initiatives. Glove-making was being developed in Cambridge as a new wartime enterprise industry. It was introduced by Rutherfords on King's Parade and the price, quality and workmanship of the 'Cam glove' was equal to any. The new industry provided additional employment for girls as well. W.K. Vauser at the Glove Warehouse also gained a reputation for 'reliable gloves'.

A Cambridgeshire herb-growers' association were meeting the demand for medicinal herbs as well as those used in cooking and had already marketed a ton of fresh and dried herbs. There was also a new venture by the Great Eastern Railway to promote an egg and poultry industry. A promotional 'egg train' came to Cambridge to give demonstrations of how this industry would work and be profitable. The idea was that smallholders should keep three hens per acre of their holding. If three fowls per acre were maintained, the scheme would give extra egg supply, more chickens for consumption when their laying days were finished, and poultry manure, which could be sold for profit as well. The eggs and poultry project received much support and the Great Eastern train travelled around the East Anglian region to publicise the idea and gain further support. This was entirely in keeping with the idea of self-sufficiency and combating 'abnormal increases in the price of food'.

The government had been advised to guarantee a minimum price for wheat but had failed to do so and the country was now vulnerable to shortages. It was feared that a loaf of bread would soon cost 1/- (£3). There was a food prices protest meeting held at Cambridge Co-operative Hall in Burleigh Street along with demands that 'profiteers should be crucified', and that the government should offer the public protection from them. The government was also being urged to take counter-measures to encourage the production, transport and marketing of home-grown foods. It was generally felt that there was 'official apathy and indifference' towards the question of food costs and that the problem could be solved by fixing food prices and perhaps some rationing. However, 'as profits come in the door, patriotism flies out the window', lamented one Cambridge citizen, while at a Cottenham meeting on the same subject someone asked plaintively: 'Why doesn't God just stop the war?'

Locally, both borough and county councils were distracted by the question of care and detention of the mentally ill. Finally, it was certified that the workhouses should look after their own while Fulbourn and Chesterton asylums cared for others, but none of these was considered suitable for the care of mentally ill soldiers and sailors. Fulbourn had both soldier and sailor inmates at one point, but it had been decided the asylum there was not really a proper place for their treatment.

Many mental problems for the troops were caused by the use of mustard (chlorine) gas, which attacked the nervous system. The introduction of this chemical warfare in 1915 hardened dislike of the Germans into hatred for many people. A 'hidden plague of STDs' at Addenbrookes was now of 'enormous prevalence' and there was much discussion of how curable STDs were. Cherryhinton Hospital had over 800 patients suffering from STDs and Barnwell (ironically the site of a former leper colony whose little chapel still survives) also had a number of patients suffering from STDs. The main one was syphilis, which could result in madness if untreated.

Meanwhile, the king visited the troops in France to offer encouragement and moral support. The official film of his visit, *The King with his Armies in France*, was shown at both the Victoria and Playhouse cinemas, and the Victoria showed a number of other war films as well including *The Defence of Verdun*, *French Advance on the Somme*, and General Smut's *Big Push*. However, there were still heavy casualties returning from the Western Front and morale at home was low. Christmas this year would 'definitely not be as usual'. Despite this there was a further increase in war weddings, and the Red Cross raised £700 (around £42,400) from a 'monster jumble sale'. Parcels of food including cakes, plum puddings and alcohol rations as Christmas treats, plus comforts and tobacco, were sent to the soldiers spending Christmas at the front. Great Eastern Railway provided free buffets for travelling soldiers and sailors at Liverpool Street Station. The farmers, still aggrieved over the question of agricultural labour, and also by the lack of profits, killed their pigs and reduced the food supply. Eggs were now 4d (£1) each. There was a scandal when four Canadian Expeditionary Force inmates at Cherryhinton Hospital were charged with stealing two live hens worth 10/- (£30), which were later found plucked and drawn along with two skinned rabbits. The soldiers claimed that they had done it simply 'for a laugh and a feed'. Lighting restrictions were regularly contravened. Cambridge and County Trades and Labour Council vowed to paint white bands around pillars, lamp-posts, water hydrants, trees, etc, for visibility in darkness as well as painting the pavement edges white.

In view of the food problems and the farmers' stance, they also decided at the same time that they would obtain permission for people to work land attached to unoccupied dwellings or public land, so that spade cultivation of potatoes could be undertaken. Tongue in cheek, the New Theatre chose to stage *Little Tommy Tucker* as its Christmas pantomime. Although in the end there were a number of Christmas Day meals, events and entertainments, jollity was muted. In the hospitals it was 'a quiet holiday but the food was good'. The university provided Christmas treats for the 150 Serbian boy refugees alone without their families and friends. Selwyn College held a Christmas Day service.

Trinity College provided Christmas lunch and Downing College provided a Christmas tea.

In mid-December, there was a new government with a strong war cabinet that included Dr Addison as minister of munitions and Lord Robert Cecil as minister of blockade. David Lloyd George was now the prime minister and he appointed Andrew Bonar Law, a very capable man, as chancellor. Arthur Balfour was foreign secretary, Lord Derby became war secretary, Sir Edward Carson the first lord of the admiralty, and a food controller was appointed in the person of Lord Devonport. The war was costing the country £7,500,000 (£450,000,000) per day and a war savings committee was set-up to try and raise some of this enormous amount of money. There were also pleas for further economies on a grand scale. The Germans had put forward peace proposal initiatives after the horror and carnage of the Somme, but the government saw this as a propaganda trick and absolutely refused to even discuss peace until the 'military autocracy of Prussia is overthrown'. Bertrand Russell, a pacifist philosopher and a lecturer at Trinity College, was roundly censured for writing to the American president urging peace, and the Bishop of Ely condemned the suggestion of peace on the grounds that it 'would be an unrighteous ending to a righteous war'. It seemed that there would be a lot more fighting and a lot more people would have to die first.

This was a dispiriting and sobering thought for those at home facing a third Christmas without loved ones in increasingly difficult times, and they hoped desperately that 1917 would finally bring an end to the war.

CHAPTER 4

1917

New Year was a very quiet affair 'without ringing bells, soaring rockets and the clamour of the crowd … and no midnight rushes to King's Parade'. It followed the pattern of Christmas when, the local paper reported sadly, there were 'only fifteen Christmas Day bathers in the Cam which was overflowing its banks and running rapidly'. The war expenditure was now running at £6,000,000 (£300,000,000) per day, of which only a third was recouped from taxes. The balance was to be raised through war loans and war bonds, which Lloyd George described as 'silver bullets'. The borough council and the university collaborated to invest £10,000 (£500,000) each in the war loan. There was an immediate and serious need as well to begin growing as much food domestically as possible. The aim was to become self-sufficient and to cut down on expense, import duties and the constant threat to merchant shipping from the German U-boats. War department land was now under cultivation and farmers were urged to grow oats for army use. Wheat was essential and the government wanted millions of acres that had previously been arable land to be restored to arable use. A plague of rats was currently attacking existing wheat supplies and in Cambridge and the county 1d (25p) was paid per rat head for their destruction.

There was also the question of barley. Barley was used to make both bread and beer and soon grain shortages were going to force a choice. In

Zeppelin over Emmanuel Street 1915
(courtesy of Cambridge Local Studies)

addition, there was a move to revive pig-keeping as a cottage industry since 'the cottager's pig has been almost legislated out of existence'. Besides, there was a problem, now that meat could be frozen, with some suppliers keeping it in storage until prices could be forced up. As Lloyd George had said, this was a war about profit not principle. In any case, it had been decided, after a meeting of Cambridge and District Butchers' Association, that meat prices should be fixed. The price of cattle was currently high and few butchers were making any profit at all.

Cambridge Waterworks Company was losing rates revenue due to the number of unoccupied houses. Many families had simply doubled-up while their men were away fighting because neither rent nor rates had been reduced and many dwellings had simply become unaffordable. There was also loss of revenue from lodging house allowances as many lodging houses were running on empty. The economic effects of the war were encouraging both Cambridge and its university to think about the future. It was generally agreed that more industries needed to be established that were not based on the university and that the construction trades needed work, funding and promotion.

One industry, however, which was growing and whose products were in great demand was that of scientific instrument-making. When the university had established its science Tripos, teaching staff had to make their own apparatus as there were no facilities for doing so in the town. The workshop of the university's Department of Mechanisms then began making scientific apparatus in 1878. One of its students, Robert Fulcher, later set-up his own scientific instrument-making business, in which he was later joined by Horace Darwin, the youngest son of Charles Darwin. In 1880, William Pye became the foreman, and the following year Darwin, in partnership with Albert George Dew-Smith (an engineer from Trinity College), purchased the business, and the Cambridge Scientific Instrument Company was born. The 'rocking microtome', used to 'cut thin sections of wax-embedded materials of either animal or plant origin', was possibly the company's most well-known product. Others included the Callendar resistance thermometer, the Callendar recorder, used with electrical resistance thermometers, and a CO_2 recorder for use at high temperatures. In 1898, William Pye left and established his own scientific instrument-making company, which ultimately became the Pye Group. Successful ventures like this served to emphasise the fact that the university might do well to make room for more brains and less wealth. Recently there had been grumblings that Cambridge was 'over burdened with faddism and cranks which stalk arrogantly over us'.

Rent and rates were still rising steadily as well as food and fuel prices. Separation allowances and pensions were generally inadequate and slow to arrive. One naval wife found that she was expected to keep herself and her five children on 23s (about £57) for a week. Discharged soldiers discovered that the country was very far from the 'promised land fit for heroes', and numbers of them became 'gentlemen of the road'. This disappointed social reformers, who had hoped that the tramp nuisance was a thing of the past, and irritated many inhabitants of Cambridge and the county.

The allotments scheme in the town was growing slowly and the government began requisitioning land under DORA. This move caused more controversy among the county farmers and they accused the government of being land thieves. The government retorted that generally continental farmers were more efficient and productive than British farmers. Seed and feeding stuffs for livestock were urgently needed and the government appealed to market gardeners to grow potatoes under glass to deter blight and pests. Farmers were asked to concentrate on grain crops, wool, hay, milk, fat stock and to turn over fields previously devoted to mustard or celery crops to growing corn or potatoes. Allotment holders began to grow a wide variety of vegetables ranging from carrots, onions, beans and parsnips to marrows, spinach, lettuce and tomatoes.

The licensing restrictions were still causing grief and soldiers were regularly arrested for drinking spirits, although the town had a good sobriety record (245 pubs but only nineteen convictions for drunkenness), but the Star Brewery in the town was also feeling the pinch and declared themselves 'tired of light beers'. The problem now was the question of barley supplies and were they to be used for beer or bread.

Transportation was another problem. The railways were denuded by the number of trains, trucks and carriages sent to the continent for use at the front, leaving inadequate rolling-stock on the Home Front.

The Cambridge Regiment had been highly praised for their boldness and gallantry in action but 135 of them were now prisoners-of-war. They were entitled to three food parcels per fortnight and the cost to the town and county was £3,000 (£150,000) per annum. Foods were sent in rotation. The first parcel might contain sausages, jam, beans, dates, tea, milk, sugar, dripping, biscuits, herrings, soups, condiments or curry powder. The second would have biscuits, cocoa, milk, raisins, bacon, cheese, chocolate, mackerel, syrup, Quaker oats, Oxo and soup, while the third parcel would be made up of rations, tea, salmon, sugar, milk, honey, dripping, vegetables, nuts, fruitcake. Relatives could send some tobacco or cash. Clothing sent included trousers, tunics, caps, underwear, boots, towels, handkerchiefs and gloves. Cambridgeshire County Council gave the use of an office, store room and packing room rent-free for sending the parcels, but money had to be raised to cover the cost of food, packaging, printing and postage costs. Prisoners-of-war could send home two letters per month and one postcard a week.

It was a hard life but better than those of their comrades daily facing the bullets and gassing and muddy hell of the trenches. More and more men were needed at the front to replace those lost, killed or injured, and this was now making serious inroads into available male labour. Seventy-eight out of 105 male Co-operative employees in Cambridge had enlisted and so had large numbers of council employees, shop assistants, drivers, manual workers, agricultural labourers, professional men and members of the police force. Thirty-four out of fifty-six policemen in the borough were of military age, but all fifty-six had attested. To maintain law and order, eighty-three special constables were drafted from among men the army had rejected on grounds of age, physical shortcomings or medical problems. They were sworn-in, given basic training and, grudgingly, some items of uniform such as overcoats and serge tunics. But the public in Cambridge resented them just as much as the public did in other towns and cities. The feeling was that they were not 'real policemen', just upstarts giving themselves airs and graces, and many resisted discipline or arrest by 'specials'.

The university, keen to do their bit as well, had a force of 134 men sworn-in as special constables who could also act as firemen in case of necessity. Up on the Gog Magog hills, Cambridge Volunteers were receiving instruction and training in bomb-throwing in a network of trenches used by cadets quartered in Cambridge. On Friday, 13 April,

Cambridge cadets took part in a series of manoeuvres known as the Battle of the Gogs in which real tanks and aeroplanes were used, and this was the talk of the town. A film of it was made and later shown at the Victoria Cinema, which also included the cadets' march along Kings Parade and their 'knife and fork drill' held in the Great Hall at Trinity College.

Lloyd George had now turned his attention to the pressing problems of food production and shortages. He ordered the food controller to fix the price of potatoes on a national scale and Cambridgeshire farmers were instructed by the Board of Agriculture to grow more potatoes and more corn. Sharp frosts had already affected the wheat crops, although oats had remained stable. Seventy-five German prisoners-of-war, housed in Linton, were allotted to help with the work. Due to the problems with agricultural labour, much land, especially 'heavy' land (clay soils, etc) had been run down and neglected. Ditches and watercourses had not been cleaned out or maintained. Farmers were complaining about the new minimum agricultural wage of 30/- (£75) for a ten-hour day and six-day week. Previously, farmers claimed, many benefits had not been expressed in cash. The farmers also felt that labourers were only working an eight-hour day, eking out duties and slowing productivity, and in April they staged an ultimately futile protest strike against the new minimum wage and shorter hours. They were not any happier about having German prisoners-of-war working the land either, but at least the labour was free and, in any case, the government was not receptive to their objections. The government was also proposing, under the terms of DORA, to take the Lammas lands in Newnham for war allotments, and a group of 'willing wounded workers' from St Chad's Red Cross Hospital cultivated vacant ground near the hospital for their own allotments. A series of lectures was held for allotment-holders on how to grow specific items, what grew best and where, rotation of crops, types of manuring, etc. Potatoes required a lot of attention and could be difficult. Any crop could be planted after potatoes but cauliflowers should not be planted after Brussels sprouts. It was suggested that half the available allotment land should be used to grow potatoes and the other half used for cabbages, root vegetables, peas and beans, the latter two of which needed careful cultivation.

A motor ploughshare was demonstrated in Cambridge and there was local promotion of both steam and motor ploughing. Former ploughmen were still being repatriated for ploughing work.

Food shortages and restrictions were increasing. Fulbourn Asylum, which was still taking mentally ill military casualties, reduced its daily rations (recommended by the food controller) of meat to 8oz (approx. 250g) and bread to 10oz (approx. 315g). Porridge was introduced for breakfast and lunch was reduced from cocoa, bread and cheese to just a cup of cocoa. The Cambridge Workhouse was struggling with increased food costs and at one point used bad black potatoes that were completely inedible. Bread, meat and sugar rations were also well below official allowances and one-course one-pot meals were advocated.

There was a 'battle of the kitchens' appeal to women to help fight and win the war against the Germans through good housekeeping and voluntary rationing. Pleas were made to reduce the use of bread and flour. War bread, a dark bread made from barley and other grains, was not liked, although it was a little cheaper. The king, anxious to show that everyone was affected by shortages, ordered members of the royal family to eat only two slices of bread per day and then asked his subjects to do the same. This seemed to have little effect in Cambridge where only 8 per cent of the population heeded his request. There were also sugar shortages and problems with milk supplies. Queues at butchers, bakers and grocers grew steadily and women would queue for hours in some cases just to obtain basic provisions. In an attempt to relieve the situation and make some attempt at fair shares for all, a new venture, the Food Culture Society, was established in Cambridge whose aims were:

• education of rural people in the production of food
• co-operative purchasing principles
• co-operative distribution of produce.

The society also attempted to persuade Cambridge bee-keepers to join with them, but the bee-keepers were not keen as it was a new society that might not know its markets. The major event in the spring of 1917, however, was the formation and recruitment drive for the Women's Land Army, which was part of the National Service scheme for war work. Women could apply and sign forms at their local post office. They were then summoned to appear before a joint committee of employment exchange and district selection/allocation for interview. If accepted the woman underwent a medical examination and was then registered and placed under the care of the district village registrar for the village where she would work. Women entered at three levels:

Land Army workers at the harvest in Bottisham c1917
(courtesy of Cambridge Local Studies)

- if sufficiently skilled she would go straight to a farm as a paid worker
- if suitable she received a 16/- (£40) per week bursary and was placed on a farm for training
- if she required four weeks basic training she would go to a centre with expenses paid.

There was also an appeal for males aged 18–61 to show patriotism and volunteer to form a male register of village workers who could be asked to undertake work of national importance anywhere in Britain. There would be a minimum wage of 25/- (just over £62) per week with a possible subsistence allowance. Framlingham & Eastern Counties Egg and Poultry Co-operative had been founded as well, encouraged by the Great Eastern egg train venture, and would cover poultry-keeping, egg-production and distribution throughout Norfolk, Suffolk, Essex and Cambridgeshire. The egg trade revival was welcomed by everyone.

To the dismay of many, Reach Fair, held near Cambridge, was on the point of being discontinued because it was regarded as 'frivolous expenditure' in wartime, although it raised a great deal of money for charity and young people. The fair had been a gift from King John in 1200 and was part of ancient local tradition. Meanwhile, great efforts were made to keep the Cambridgeshire hunt going as it was felt that there was 'a duty to keep the sport alive'. However, the weather was good for the Whitsun holidays and most folk made their own amusements while the local newspaper managed to forget the war for a brief instant, waxing lyrical about spring and the re-birth of nature:

Nature is rioting in leaf and flower ... woods and hedgerows are gay with lilac, laburnum, hawthorn, chestnut and rhododendron ... brilliant green meadows ... are prodigally besprinkled with buttercups and daisies, and ... pale yellow cowslips in cornfields ... are waving with up-springing crop.

Now that motoring for pleasure was forbidden due to fuel rationing, and with rail fares rising as well as train services being reduced, cyclists

*Land Army girl
in Cambridge
c1917*

were out in force again enjoying the spring sunshine. The dust created
by motor cars had deterred many of them from venturing on the roads.

Cherryhinton Road Hospital established a programme of Sunday
concerts, which proved to be popular. Many just enjoyed walking along
'the backs', the name given to the banks of the Cam behind the colleges.

Cambridge Baby Week was held in early June to promote safeguarding
the health of mothers and babies and focused on early years care and
monitoring, weight, feeding, health, hygiene, nursing and practical

mothercraft. Infant mortality stood at sixty-nine per 1,000 in the county and seventy-two per 1,000 in the borough. Although high by twenty-first-century standards, the figures were quite low for the times. In one of the northern mill-towns, infant mortality was 440 per 1,000, almost 50 per cent. There was still a high number of diphtheria and whooping cough cases, which usually proved fatal and, of course, the ever-present TB. One Cambridge newspaper reader decided that 'high infant mortality is the result of women being unable to deal with both home affairs and external matters and therefore it would help if female emancipation were dismissed', but generally there was a growing awareness that the generation lost to the war needed to be replaced and the baby week was dubbed 'week of the rising generation' by the press.

Elsewhere, though, the picture was much less rosy. There was a rise in petty juvenile crime in Cambridge deemed to be mainly due to absent fathers, working mothers and watching the wrong kind of films in the cinemas:

> *Every reformatory school in the country is full (mostly of boys) due to crime and disorder among young people ... due to absent fathers and mothers not strong enough morally or physically to discipline their children ... school discipline is ineffective and although we do not want to make our Jacks and Jills dull boys and girls ... restraining influence is required if we are not to become a nation of hooligans.*

A century on little has changed, but the punishments in 1917 were more severe. Magistrates regularly ordered the use of the birch and miscreants were publicly whipped. Social values and a sense of community were also more pronounced, which meant offenders often brought shame on both themselves and their families as well.

Teachers, who were traditionally paid low wages, were fighting for salary increases and a war bonus due to the rapidly rising costs of living. In Cambridge there was outrage that the NUT should fight the teachers' case for them and in the council chambers. On the continent, teachers were valued as 'persons of learning and essential pillars of the community', and were paid accordingly, whereas in Britain teaching, like nursing, was seen as a vocation that didn't merit much salary. Besides, it was believed that teachers entered the profession mainly for the long holidays they received. Most teachers, then as now, insisted that was very far from the case. Council workers, gas workers, policemen, public transport workers were all receiving war bonuses, and often were on higher wages than teachers. In the case of police, a complicated scheme was proposed to pay part of the war bonus based on the price of bread, which led to it becoming known as the bread bonus.

The great irony was, and it was not lost on the troops, that the main body of folk who did not receive any kind of war bonus were those actually fighting the war, the soldiers, sailors and airmen. There was a large airfield out at Duxford, although in 1917 the average life expectancy of a British airman was said to be eleven days. The Cambridge School of Flying and Aerodynamics always had immediate vacancies for the training of pilots and aircraft engineers. There was a story of an enterprising German pilot who hung a red light on a rope 200ft (just over 60m) beneath his plane as a decoy for anti-aircraft fire. The light would be hit and go out so that those on the ground believed they had hit the plane while he escaped.

Cambridge Red Cross was doing sterling work. They now maintained sixteen auxiliary hospitals in connection with the First Eastern Hospital. In addition, they transported sick and wounded men from Cambridge Railway Station to First Eastern Hospital, organised the collection of necessary items for the sick and wounded from their depot at Bene't Street and issued them to First Eastern and the auxiliary hospitals, and they raised £1,925 6s 4d (over £96,250) towards the balance of their running costs. YMCA fundraising brought in another £300 (£15,000) for a recreation hut for wounded soldiers.

The big debate of the moment in June, however, was when the new Representation of the People Bill was passed, and its parliamentary boundary recommendations caused enormous disquiet. Cambridge borough remained unchanged but Cambridgeshire faced major changes. For these purposes the Isle of Ely was not included. Amalgamations

Pilot and plane, Cambridgeshire c1917

were made in east and west Cambridgeshire to produce two new constituencies of South Cambridgeshire and North Cambridgeshire. South Cambridgeshire stretched to Newmarket in Suffolk and North Cambridgeshire extended to the fens and the Isle of Ely. Even more controversial was the fact that the vote was to be given to women over the age of 30 and several categories of men hitherto excluded. Universal suffrage would not come until 1928, but even this much female suffrage was a major step and attracted as much criticism as it did encouragement. By way of celebration, the first female alderman, Mrs Adeane, who was the wife of the lord lieutenant for Cambridgeshire, was elected to Cambridgeshire County Council. The new MP, Sir Eric Geddes, unlike his predecessor, Almeric Paget, was a strong supporter of female suffrage.

British Summer Time had been authorised again for the summer of 1917, despite grumbles and complaints. In Cambridge it was said that schoolchildren were suffering from the daylight-saving restrictions owing to curtailment of sleeping hours due to the extra daylight. This had an effect on mothers whose rest and leisure hours were curtailed as children stayed out of doors to play while it was light. Yet children still had to get up at the same time for school and often arrived there sleepy, which, it was said, was bad for their health. The farmers also continued to grumble but the government was not listening. It was becoming essential to conserve fuel as much as possible. There was a serious shortage of coal, but Cambridge was slow to accept what more northerly towns had known for some time. There was still insistence during the summer that there would be enough coal for the coming winter in the borough, but that was simply not the case. The mining industry had been severely hit by the numbers of miners enlisting and much of the available coal was being shipped to the continent to provide fuel for trains and machinery, and warmth for the troops. Certain industries had to take precedence over private usage and requirements, but Cambridge coal merchants continued to insist until the autumn that stocks would be sufficient.

Provision of economical foodstuffs also remained a major problem and prices were still rising with meat and butter in short supply. It was insisted that all restaurants (and this would include college dining rooms) should have meatless days, although they were allowed to use fish as a substitute. Most ordinary folk could not afford usual restaurant prices so, in order to buy food in bulk cheaply and conserve fuel, communal kitchens were proposed. The idea of communal kitchens was that simple nutritious dishes could be produced very economically and that people, especially workers, could obtain at least one cooked meal a day at little cost. It would be possible to buy a two-course meal for around 1s 2d (under £3). Dishes would include soups, stews, hotpots, cottage pie, suet puddings, rice pudding, jam roly-poly, etc. Each kitchen had a functional restaurant where people could eat on the premises. Cambridge's first communal kitchen was opened on the corner of Church Street and Fitzroy Street at the end of June. Initially there was a cautious reception, which may have had something to do with personal pride, but gradually the concept of the communal kitchen gained in popularity and more were opened in Cambridge, usually serving a designated area.

At the end of August, the first ration tickets for food were issued by Lord Rhondda. Sugar supplies were to be conserved and shared equally, and prices were to be kept down. Town, gown and county had to tackle the administrative nightmare of endless regulations and the distribution of application forms, which were to be returned by 5 October. The scheme was due to begin on 30 December, and all tradesmen and their customers had to comply. Lord Rhondda's appeal for voluntary rationing led Cambridge Food Control Committee to appoint yet another committee to examine food economy and how to eliminate food wastage. Cambridge allotments were producing results. Three hundred and twelve acres had given a good crop of potatoes but the onion crop proved a failure. Carrots and turnips were passable but parsnips and artichokes had been neglected. There was, however, a glut of plums and the scouts helped to pick the fruit for the Chivers factory. Surplus fruit, and any surplus vegetables, were to be dried, bottled or pulped for consumption during the lean winter months. Children helped their parents on their own allotments and helped teachers on school allotments. It was also now proposed to commandeer another 5 acres of Lammas land for allotments and that 35

Apple harvest at Shelford 1917 (courtesy of Cambridge Local Studies)

acres of Coldham Common should be ploughed up to grow wheat.

The food control committee established in Cambridge brought with it the various problems of representation that had affected other places. Foremost was the question of Labour Party representation, but there were difficulties with the local Labour Party resulting from general annoyance that one Labour Party representative and one trades union representative had been elected to the committee. There was additional annoyance that three women were put forward but only two were elected and one of those represented the working class. The university was said to have too many representatives. It was also pointed out that no one directly involved in food supply and distribution was represented on the committee. The representation issues caused controversy for several weeks while the committee tried to deal with the problems of insufficient labour for harvesting the huge apple and plum crops and the need for extra sugar allowances to make jams.

The assassination of Grigori Rasputin on New Year's Eve 1916 was the prelude to the February 1917 revolution in Russia that ousted Tsar Nicholas II, who was held responsible for the loss of 5,000,000 Russian men in the First World War by the end of October 1916. The country withdrew from fighting after the revolution, although peace details were not finalised until early in March 1918, and as Russia was now out of the war, many of its guns were sold to Germany. The tsar's cousin, King George V, to whom the tsar bore an uncanny resemblance, was seriously worried that similar revolutionary movements, due to worsening social and economic conditions, could occur in Britain. The question of workers' war bonuses coupled with antipathy to the unions and a public 'suffering from war nerves exacerbated by profiteering, the weather and no beer' (Sir Eric Geddes MP) was making him jittery. Against the advice of the government he turned down the tsar's request for asylum, a move that resulted in the eventual execution of the Imperial family at Yekaterinburg in July 1918. George V was also acutely aware of the irony of fighting another of his cousins, the kaiser, when he himself was of pure German descent. The only non-German member of the immediate line of royal descent since George I ascended the throne in 1714 had been George's mother, Queen Alexandra, and she was from Denmark, a close neighbour of Germany. He was married to a German princess and his surname, Saxe-Coburg-Gotha, was the same as that of his grandfather, Prince Albert, the husband of Queen Victoria, who was herself of German descent. George couldn't do much about his family lineage but he could make a statement about his British loyalties and patriotism. Consequently, on 17 July, he issued a royal proclamation, read from the steps of every town hall in the country:

Now, therefore, We, out of Our Royal Will and Authority, do hereby declare and announce that as from the date of this Our Royal Proclamation, Our House and Family shall be styled and known as the House and Family of Windsor, and that all the descendants in the male line of Our said Grandmother, Queen Victoria, who are subjects of this realm ... shall bear the said Name of Windsor.

All the king's British relatives gave up their German names and titles and the royal family today (2015) still bears the name of Windsor. Among the most well-known of his family was yet another of George's cousins, Prince Louis of Battenberg, who had been forced to resign as first sea lord because of anti-German sentiments. He took on the name and title of Louis Mountbatten, 1st Marquess of Milford Haven, and was the father of Louis Mountbatten, 1st Earl Mountbatten of Burma, who, in the Second World War, became affectionately known simply as 'Monty'.

There were fears that Germany could still take over the world after the war, but on economic terms. Both Germany and Austria had been buying up raw supplies and accumulating resources for years. An Imperial Trade Policy was therefore drawn up so that Britain could take charge of its destiny and resist German economic domination. There were a dozen main points, many of which affected Cambridge, its university and its county:

1. steps to be taken for stimulation of production of foodstuffs, raw materials and manufactures
2. wider range of customs duties
3. British capital for British industry and British labour

4. preferential tariffs for Allies
5. full utilisation and development of national and imperial resources
6. agricultural system that secures fullest development of natural land resources
7. reconstruction of British industry and the labour question
8. development of sources of supply of raw materials
9. production of an adequate food supply
10. control and conservation of natural resources
11. reform of 'Alien' and 'Naturalisation' Acts
12. better organisation of distributional industries and measures against 'dumping'

However, interest and discussion of these proposals were overshadowed by the third anniversary of the war as hostilities entered their fourth year. In 1916, the Officers Cadets Corps had been initiated to train 'rankers' as officers, and two battalions were allocated to Cambridge. Officers and men were housed in various colleges – the 2nd Battalion, having its headquarters at Pembroke, and the 15th at Trinity College. This year the 22nd Battalion had been based in Cambridge as well. As a result of these corps, many commissions were granted to labour and home service battalions. Recruits filled nearly empty colleges, stimulating trade and saving the town from 'moral and material depression'. They were inspected by King George V when he paid a visit to the First Eastern Hospital and were an important boost to the town.

It was also the third anniversary of the formation of the Cambridge Volunteers, but the battalion was now low in numbers. A minimum of 600 men were needed for the battalion to remain properly active. The Cambridgeshire regiment had received much praise for skills and gallantry when fighting in France and Flanders, although casualties remained high, and the Territorials also received commendations for bravery, but again casualties were high. The county had 781 dead, 1,325 wounded, 147 prisoners-of-war, and 182 missing. The university had lost nearly 2,000 men, the town far more. First Eastern was caring for an average of 800 wounded men at any one time. Despite this, the third anniversary was little marked in Cambridge; although there was a war service held in Great St Mary's. Everything was just too raw.

Generally, morale was low and there were threats of strikes and industrial unrest everywhere. Cambridge was threatened with a rail strike by workers wanting the same pay for shorter hours. The unions were generally condemned and strikes were held to be unpatriotic in the extreme, but behind it all were the problems of high rents, rising fuel costs, inflated food prices and blatant profiteering. Cambridge families were experiencing difficulties in obtaining adequate 'meat and wheat' rations and ration lists had been issued for 1918.

Meanwhile, the 'beer or bread' question still hung over barley supplies. Thrift was constantly advocated and 12,000,000 new war savings certificates were issued. The War Savings Committee wanted the public to finance the war by putting their savings into war bonds and war certificates. In Cambridge, the borough war savings committee had initially covered the county and the Isle of Ely as well, but separate associations were now formed. There were thirty-seven war savings associations in the town with each contributor paying on average £1.07 (around £52). Appeals were made to businessmen to supply finance through war bonds, and it was at this point that Oxford and Cambridge, deprived of their boat race for the third year in succession, decided to hold a bond race. It was a novel idea which created great interest and the Cambridge and Oxford Bond Race resulted in daily telegraphic exchanges of results. Eventually Oxford won, but Cambridge raised a very considerable sum as well. Friendly Societies also contributed both men and money, 'fighters and fighting funds', to the war effort while the boy scouts and the YMCA, aided by school cadets and flag-day collectors, undertook 'good works', fundraising and entertainments as their contribution. However, there was yet another political row brewing and it involved the borough council.

Since 1872, the local Conservatives and Liberals had, by tacit agreement, put forward candidates for the Cambridge mayoralty, and in every seventh year the university proposed a candidate. This year the Liberals had caused enormous upset and offence by asking the university to propose a mayoral candidate instead of choosing a mayor from among their own party, and doing so without asking the Conservatives for their views. The proposed new mayor was the Reverend E.C. Pearce, Master of Corpus Christi, who was also the first clerical candidate for the mayoralty. Local Conservatives were further annoyed by discussion of the forthcoming mayor while the present mayor still had three months to run in office and termed this greatly disrespectful to the current incumbent. This did not prevent them, however, from tinkering with the mayoral selection and causing yet more irritations. In the wake of all this political squabbling, a manifesto was issued by the new National Party, who hoped that 'the better elements of the Unionists (Conservatives), Radicals (Liberals) and Labour Parties would agree to its five major aims:

- failure of old party system, which should be replaced
- vigorous prosecution of the war to a victorious conclusion
- reform of the British constitution, with honest administration and no sale of honours
- union of empire and social union at home, with fair wages and fair profits, no class differentiation and equal opportunities for all
- defence after the war, with decent demobs of soldiers and sailors

For the time being, however, the reality remained that the 'no opposition party rule to the war government resulted in endless old gasbags and windbags spouting on ... filling 60 columns of Hansard in one day, 30 of the columns belonging to just two MPs'.

Sir Robert Baden-Powell gave a lecture on *Has the War been worth it?* He seemed to think so because 'as a nation Britain was drifting materially, sliding down morally and physically ... and the crisis has pulled us up and pulled us together ... revolution or evolution ... the desire for self-expression, general raising of the standard of living, for giving everyone a chance ... but the danger is too much self-expression by too few with too little thought for others'. Could the war help democracy? 'Yes, if it means government by the people for the people, not internecine struggle for sectional advantages regardless of national welfare.'

Some wondered if 'state control was actually becoming a menace, a corruption of liberties, injurious and demoralising; with restriction rationing, price fixing, fiscal changes, nationalisation of railways'.

Cambridge Red Cross began promoting its prize draws in September, which had always proved a good method of raising money, but to the amazement of many the Chapter of Cambridge Deanery objected on religious grounds that it was an illegal lottery which encouraged gambling. Initially, Cambridge and the Isle of Ely Red Cross believed that it was a storm in a teacup that would blow over, but a few days later a legal injunction forced them to abandon their prize draws altogether. Subscriptions had to be returned on application and the Red Cross lost £1,000 (over £50,000). This finally caused some members of the clergy to feel a little guilty about their unremitting stance and they offered to compensate Cambridge Red Cross. Unsurprisingly, the Red Cross ignored them. Enough damage had been done. The organisation now appealed for funds and helpers as a matter of urgency. The local prisoner-of-war fund needed £10,500 (£525,000) to support Cambridge prisoners overseas.

It was a grim autumn. There was a still a great deal of discontent among the town corporation employees over wages and war bonuses. Pubs were closing early due to the poor quality of the beer. A milk and butter shortage was feared for the winter and milk prices were still rising. Student figures for the new academic year at the university were very low, even among medical students. Cambridge Town Council had to be prevented by the Local Government Board from charging £10 (over £500) in rent for the use of a room by Cambridge War Pensions Committee, from which they carried out their administrative work. The committee was being dilatory at best in dealing with war pensions, and the continuing muddle was causing some real cases of hardship. Many felt badly let down.

Meanwhile, the War Pensions Committee was accused of 'subterranean proceedings', and there were a number of proposed staff changes. There were also issues with advisory committee difficulties and civil liabilities grants. In addition, there was the scandal of issuing 'shoddy suits and red neckerchiefs' to discharged soldiers, making them look like casual or itinerant labourers instead of being 'given attire becoming to their position'. There were difficulties with supplies of boots as well, so there was the suggestion that clogs should be worn instead.

The recently formed Cambridge Chamber of Commerce discussed ideas for new factories and industries in the town, which would mean an immediate need for the provision of working class homes – a need that already existed. A fledgling diamond-cutting industry for disabled soldiers was begun, but sadly did not succeed, partly due to a lack of funding and proper training. A few smiles were raised, however, by a request from the director of propellant supplies to collect horse chestnuts, both in the town and the county. Cambridge wits assumed that Britain might be challenging Germany to a terminal conker fight, but the reality was more prosaic. Chestnuts were used in the production of acetone, which in turn was used in the production of cordite. Cordite is 'a smokeless powder used as a propellant in small arms ammunition and artillery'. It has a longer range than gunpowder and does not obscure gunners' views.

There was a show exhibition of 'wonderful produce' from the borough allotments held at the Corn Exchange in September. The seasonal crop reports had been varied. Wheat was 'under average' while barley was 'just OK' but oats were 'poor' and beans 'rotten bad'. Potatoes and mangolds had yielded good crops, so too had turnips and swedes, although some damage had been caused by turnip fly. The Women's Land Service Corps had provided 'strong women' for the potato harvest, fruit-picking and general unskilled agricultural work in the county. The Food Production Department now wanted another 3,000,000 acres under corn, potato and mangold production for 1918. Isle of Ely bulb growers were told to plough and plant 25 per cent of their land with wheat and to sow wheat or oats between the rows of bulbs on a further 25 per cent of their land. Bread was a little cheaper and there was large-scale conservation of surplus fruit and vegetables developing rapidly and effectively at the Cambridge depot for dealing with surplus plums. Extra sugar was allocated for making blackberry, apple or marrow jams, although the making of rhubarb jam was not allowed. Spring rhubarb is better because, in autumn, frosts can increase the level of toxins in the stems and also 'woody stems' are not suitable.

Cambridge Borough had almost found itself left out of the jam sugar allocations. Cottenham, a large fruit producing area, with a population of 2,500 people, had received 4 tons of sugar, while Cambridge, with a population of 60,000, had received just 5 tons, which prompted great protest. The situation was finally resolved with a warning that the 'yardstick' should not be fruit production but preservation for one's own use. Amazingly, 1,000 applications for sugar were incorrectly completed even by those with a good education and there were disgruntled murmurings about the sugar allocations for colleges.

The Food Control Committee was flexing its muscles and held a meeting with all food tradesmen owning motor or horse-delivery vans. There was to be co-operation and economy in transport, no overlapping of delivery routes, small district limits were to be set, distribution was only to take place between one and three times a week, not daily, and perishables were to be given priority. Bread deliveries were to be abolished and milk deliveries reduced to one per day, and delivery charges were illegal. Potato sales licences were also issued.

The Ministry of Food prohibited sales of cattle feeding cake and meal except by specific licence. There was to be less meat and bread per person, and tea, cereals, butter, margarine and lard were to be rationed. Maximum meat retail prices for beef, pork and mutton were published by the food committee. Butchers feared low prices would curtail the meat trade and forecast 'a meat famine', especially of mutton. They were making little profit now that livestock and dead meat prices had been fixed. Butchers said they couldn't sell at present price levels and some feared they would have to close their shops. One butcher explained a major problem was that consumers only wanted to pay for meat, not bones, while the butchers were forced to pay for whole carcasses. There had been no increase in the price of milk so dairymen were faced with the same quandary as butchers. The gap between purchase and selling prices was too small for them to survive commercially.

Long queues outside tea and provisions shops were now a regular sight in Cambridge but were regarded as 'a necessary evil', as rationing of foodstuffs would happen soon. A big part of the problem seemed to be the lack of self-regulation. Despite many pleas to the contrary folk were buying as much as they could rather than what they needed. Government suggestions that affluent shoppers buy the more expensive cuts of meat and leave cheaper cuts for the poor were being ignored. There was also the problem of profiteering and many foodstuffs were withheld until the price was forced up. Cambridge was interested in the idea of food control, and cookery economy weeks were held in mid-December at the Milton and East Road cookery schools and at the Morley Memorial Cookery Kitchen. They lasted three days. Day one concentrated on soups and cereals, day two on dinners at 2d or 3d (40p or 60p), day three on vegetable cookery and cold meat cookery. Admission was free and demonstrations were based on current rationing.

Christmas promised to be a subdued affair and there was a big economy drive aimed at Christmas presents with lots of useful suggestions. Shops were to close on 25, 26 and 27 December for the Christmas holidays. The royal family chose their Christmas cards with care. The king's card was a painting of the Grand Fleet in the Battle of Jutland, which took place on 31 May 1916. Queen Mary's card showed a royal wooing of 1420. Queen Alexandra (the queen mother) depicted the lady of the lamp (Florence Nightingale) on her card and the Prince of Wales (later Edward VIII) had the caption on his card read 'Onward! The Golden Age is not behind but before us!'

Women worked in the post office to deliver all the Christmas mail despite the fact that noticeably fewer cards were posted this year. Matthew and Son of Trinity Street decided to splash out and advertised 'grocery; cakes; bons-bons; plum puddings; mince pies; wine'. This was somewhat contrary to government and food control committee advice but it was an antidote to the general feeling of gloom. By contrast, Cambridge University and Town Gas Light Company raised prices, urged fuel economy and ceased hiring out gas cookers or gas fires. Fires were not to be on at full strength, use of hot water was to be reduced to a minimum, the number of rooms heated and/or lit were to be limited, and the use of gas for cooking was to be reduced. One-pot meals should be cooked or a mat placed over one ring so that several dishes could be cooked using minimal gas. Train services were greatly reduced and there was no guarantee of being able to reach particular destinations. In Cambridge, as in most other places, passengers were advised not to travel at all over Christmas as preference would be given to soldiers on leave.

Slogans like 'Saving food means feeding the guns', 'Don't be greedy. Grow your own and buy less', 'Dig for Victory' became common and SOS (Save or Starve) Weeks were held for economy. Christmas food queues were badly regulated with lots of tricks, evasions and subterfuge. Queues in Petty Cury became dangerous so the stocks of margarine were moved to the Corn Exchange. The butchers suspended their threatened 'lock-out' for Christmas, which was a welcome move, but retailers were losing more than just the cost of sales.

The Victoria Cinema's choice of Christmas film was, appropriately enough, *Jack and the Beanstalk*. Christmas dinners and entertainments were provided for wounded troops and children; the Cambridge Workhouse, local institutions and hospitals. This year roast pork was substituted for roast turkey or roast beef and jam roly poly was served in place of the traditional Christmas pudding. Hospital wards and children's homes were gaily decorated.

Trinity College gave the Serbian boy-refugees a quiet simple dinner in college. There was also the ongoing spectacle of military weddings, steadily rising in numbers as times became more desperate.

The highlight of Christmas Day, however, was the annual Christmas morning tradition of swimming in the Cam, despite a hard frost followed by snow. There were still high numbers of casualties from the fronts. Three Cambridge brothers were wounded and two Fulbourn bothers were killed. An Australian cadet died from influenza, a fore-runner of the 1918 pandemic. The local newspaper wrote despairingly of Christmas 1917, 'Peace, where shall it be found? Goodwill, where does it exist?' Folk tried to retain their faith, hope and charity, but it was a tremendous effort in the face of the depression and the bitterness at the prolonged fighting, hardships and the restrictions of daily life. So many deaths and still no end in sight, 1917 in Cambridge was a year 'which closed without many regrets'.

CHAPTER 5

1918

On New Year's Day a Central Kitchens Committee was formed in Cambridge and given a grant by the town council to build on the experimental work of the first communal kitchen in Fitzroy Street. The idea of communal kitchens was excellent but too many folk were treating them as tea and cooked meat shops instead of a place where they could eat good, simple nourishing meals. However the Cambridge one was doing well and a town council grant of £400 (£17,400) was given for another one at St Luke's Vicarage in Chesterton. Fitzroy Street had already opened a large dining room adjacent to the kitchen and the Chesterton kitchen had a dining room as well. Chesterton also provided dinners for Chesterton schoolchildren during the winter and meals for employees of the Cambridge Scientific Instrument Company. A third kitchen, Newtown Kitchen, opened in Cheshunt College and supplied a restaurant on Hills Road, a depot at Newnham, dinners for numbers of Serbian students and, in addition, it catered for Australian officers who were on a special course at Cheshunt College. The three kitchens were popular and did good trade. The profits were used to set-up a fourth kitchen in Romsey Town to serve the adjacent districts. The kitchens continued to operate even after the war was over because continuing food and fuel shortages rendered them necessary. The food rations were adequate in quality if not in quantity. A typical adult weekly ration of food was:

- 2oz tea (approximately 16 tea bags)
- 8oz (250g) sugar
- 4 pints milk
- 1 loaf (large brown, 2lb in weight, which is that of an average large uncut loaf)
- 4oz (125g) butter
- 4oz (125g) cheese (Cheddar, Cheshire or Lancashire)
- 4 eggs
- 2oz bacon (works out at 2 rashers)
- 2lb (2.5kg) meat (stewing steak, mince beef, lamb, mutton, liver, kidneys, rabbit, cow's heel)
- 1lb porridge oats
- 5lb (2.5kg) potatoes
- 1lb (500g) carrots
- 1lb (500g) onions (white)
- 2lb (1kg) green vegetables (cabbage, kale, sprouts in winter + peas, beans, etc, in summer)
- 1lb (500g) fruit (apples/pears in winter: 1lb = 2 small apples + 2 small pears, or plums and berries in summer)
- ½lb (250g) rice
- 1 small jar of preserves (marmalade, damson or summer fruit jam, apple or redcurrant jelly)

Those doing heavy manual work were allowed more meat and in special circumstances extra allowances could be made of other foods. Some northern towns applied for extra butter or margarine because workers predominantly ate sandwiches rather than cooked food for their midday meal. Everyone was now getting something of everything, shares were much fairer, and food rationing unexpectedly eradicated all the diseases of malnutrition, which included rickets, scurvy, vitamin deficiencies, stunted growth in children, stomach ailments, TB, etc. One hundred years later, the diseases of rickets and stomach ailments have made a return along with epidemics of diabetes and obesity, but today's diseases of malnutrition are due more to ignorance and laziness rather than shortages of foodstuffs.

Food rationing was introduced in stages between December 1917 and February 1918. At this point Britain was said to have only six weeks stock of wheat left. Potato bread was being promoted, pastry was mostly forbidden, and sauces without using flour were advocated. Fish and rabbit prices were fixed and no imported meat was allowed. Meatless days were firmly compulsory. Fish was permitted so restaurants could serve dishes like stuffed herring rolls as well as haricot mould, nut and cheese pie, or egg rissoles. Households were allowed to pickle 100 eggs per year.

The county villages of Willingham and Cottenham sent considerable supplies of fresh fruit and vegetables to Addenbrooke's Hospital in February. There were long queues for margarine in Burleigh Street and on Mill Road, but by July 1918 ration books were issued for butter, margarine, lard, meat and sugar. These ration books were also used for fuel rationing. Coal, coke, gas and electricity were all affected. Owing to continuing coal shortages, transport and manufacturing difficulties, there were now urgent pleas to consumers from the Cambridge University and Town Gas Works to economise even further and the gas company undertook the following measures:

• reducing the pressure
• discontinuing the supply of gas for motor vehicles
• discontinuing the supply or hire of heating stoves, cookers, water heaters, gas engines and slot meters

Finally, it was decided that consumers could not use more than 5/6 of the gas used in any corresponding quarter for 1917. Despite the repeated appeals for economy, gas consumption increased in Cambridge and townfolk seemed to ignore the pleas. A more likely scenario was the season. Christmas and New Year had been frosty before snow fell. Bitter winds blew across from the Russian steppes. East Anglia has a reputation as the coldest (and usually the driest) place in England for this reason. Snowfalls in January caused havoc and there were record floods in Grantchester, Rupert Brooke's former home. The rivers Cam and Granta were muddy and turbulent, causing floods in various parts of Cambridge, and out in the county the railway was flooded at Sawston. It was a miserable winter but, despite severe paper shortages, the Cambridge newspapers continued to publish and gamely tried to keep up spirits by publishing lists of schoolboy howlers sent in by teachers. The best of these read 'Oliver Cromwell was a very strict drunkard who fought in the Battle of Waterloo'.

The war against STDs was still causing great concern and a public meeting was held in the Guildhall to discuss this. It was felt by many that there was a conspiracy of silence over STDs, although there was really no need to hide the truth. It was a problem everywhere, just not admitted, but there were a number of hospitals around the country like Cherryhinton and Barnwell that treated STDs. Despite the popular Sunday concerts at Cherryhinton Hospital, there continued to be a great deal of resentment against its inmates as well as those at Barnwell. The mayor considered that both hospitals should be surrounded by tough barbed wire. As it was, he said, the inmates were free to go out and meet girls in Cambridge and so spread STDs.

There were problems with mismanagement of the volunteers. A number of men had joined them in 1914, but several had not undertaken either the training or continuous service required under the Volunteer Act and therefore had to leave. Those volunteers who did have their membership qualification were treated to a day on the local golf course receiving an introduction to the meaning of trench warfare. Fresh medicals would be held but those who now failed would have the option of joining A or B Sections and therefore avoid compulsory retirement from the volunteers.

There was a distinct lack of enthusiasm for National Service. Borough tribunals were still hearing appeals for exemption from war service. In the county there were continuing protests about taking labour from the land for aerodrome work at Duxford, and the labourers' cottages were being neglected. Cramped and damp they were a contributory cause for the spread of TB. There was now a firm view that these cottages 'were a curse which tied farm labourers economically and socially' and they should be abolished.

Lighting infringements by numbers of people and price infringements by butchers and dairymen, as well as those selling coffee above fixed market prices, were becoming very common. It was as if folk either couldn't care or just couldn't be bothered any more. Rat clubs were formed to deal with the growing numbers of rats, and payments were now made for a dozen tails at a time. Even hunting had to cease for reasons of economy and masters of hounds were informed that their licences would officially expire on 2 March.

Armistice Day 1918, effigy of the kaiser being taken to a bonfire on Market Hill (courtesy of Cambridge Local Studies)

Casualties continued to pour into the town and still there seemed to be no end to the war in sight. War bond sales in Cambridge slumped while the Cambridgeshire and Isle of Ely Prisoner-of-War Fund was appealing desperately for £10,500 (£456,750), being the amount needed to keep Cambridge town, university and county prisoners-of-war supplied with food and clothing. Another Oxford/Cambridge Bond Race was organised for each to raise £150,000 (£6,525,000) to fund a destroyer during Businessman's Week. Oxford won again, raising over 25 per cent more cash than Cambridge.

To add to all the woes being suffered, shortage of beer and spirits was causing unrest in the trade and among workers, as well as causing resentment and general bad temper among many elements of the population. Margarine supplies and distribution continued to cause hassle and there were complicated procedures in place for butchers selling pork offal or suet.

There seemed to be little to cheer folk. However, Lord Derby paid a visit to First Eastern in March and Princess Mary visited Cambridge in the same month and presented Land Girls badges to Land Army girls and village workers. This was followed by Anzac Day held in the town on 25 April to raise funds for prisoners-of-war. The anniversary of the landing of Australian and New Zealand troops at Gallipoli in 1915 was celebrated with a memorial service, ceremonial parade, distribution of medals, sports and a performance of the Maori war dance, the Haka.

The Cambridge Regiment had taken part in 'a great battle' on the Western Front, which lasted ten days. Although there was still heavy fighting and large numbers of casualties, there was finally a growing sense that the tide had turned. Slowly folk dared to begin thinking of a future beyond the war.

One of the most important events after the war was to hold a general election. Andrew Bonar Law, the chancellor, had unveiled his budget in April and it had hit everyone hard. Income tax had increased. Luxury tax was 2d (44/45p) in the shilling (about £2.20). Beer and spirit duties doubled. Tobacco and match duties were raised. Farmers' tax was to be doubled. Super tax was up to 4s 6d (around £7.50) in the pound (£43.50). There was a 2d (44/45p) stamp on cheques. Finally, there

Regiment return to Cambridge 1919
(courtesy of Cambridge Local Studies)

was a higher duty on sugar. Everyone winced, but the enormous war costs had to be paid for somehow. Thoughts of an election seemed to concentrate minds wonderfully. The soldiers' vote was going to be important and so too was that of newly enfranchised women.

The mayor was generally unhappy and dismayed by the morals and vandalism of boys aged 14–18 in Cambridge, but even more so about those of the girls and women. He attacked the morals of females on the streets who 'defiled clean and pure men who had resisted temptation abroad and there never was a cleaner set of men than those serving at the front'. Naturally, the church was in total agreement. He insisted that there should be women police officers to see to them and improve the state of the streets. In twenty-first century terminology, it is tempting to wonder what the mayor was on but he was simply a churchman of his time and a fairly narrow-minded one who believed that all sin was directly attributable to Eve. It explained, however, why, although women could take degrees, full membership of the university for women was opposed. It must have been difficult for women to see Belgian and Italian professors receiving full academic honours and offers of assistance while female graduates were denied the right to belong. The mayor was the master of Corpus Christi College and he would have been far from alone in his views about the female sex. However, that did not prevent the advantageous usefulness of women who now worked as scavengers for the borough council (dealing with sewage waste) and the gas works, and who were offered new classes in a variety of subjects including cobbling for mothers.

Baby Week was to be abandoned for this year and the money saved spent on skills and education classes for women. A conference was held in Cambridge on how to deal with STDs and how to treat them, and there was also a plea for equality of treatment for the sexes. At present men escaped any punishment whereas women were punished for suffering from STDs and the National Council was urged to pass a Bill that would make it a penal offence for anyone to transmit STDs either wilfully or by negligence.

Two women police officers were finally appointed to look after girls on the streets 'whose thoughtless conduct caused problems and for respectable young women who were insulted by self-appointed vigilantes if they happened to be talking to a soldier in the street. It did not necessarily mean that they had fallen from grace'.

Cambridge suffered from a spring of discontent in 1918. Apart from the vexed question of STDs and responsibility, there were fresh rises in the cost of food, fuel and postage rates, plus the ever-present rationing and restriction of everything. The Household Fuel and Lighting Order for 1918 precluded applications from lodgers for coal, gas and electricity rations. Only owners or permanent occupiers of houses could apply. The state had taken control of pensions and associated administrative duties forcing out the voluntary workers. Bureaucracy proved to be slower and more costly. Pensions were delayed and unfavourable comparisons were made between the cumbersome government pension machine and the Soldiers & Sailors Family Association, which had dealt very promptly with pension claims. There was great objection to Newmarket race goers, who were dubbed 'burly shirkers', being 'dumped' in Cambridge accommodation, wandering the streets and often making a nuisance of themselves. Racing was said to 'attract blackguards and was a big drain on police manpower'. Racing also involved gambling and betting, but the church, which had so vociferously opposed the Red Cross prize draws as encouraging gambling, remained silent in this case. Reach Fair had finally been abolished. Parker's Piece was in poor condition once more and citizens wanted it restored to its former state so that they and their children could enjoy walking and outdoor pursuits there. Co-operative employees in the town were unhappy that the Co-operative Society refused to recognise their trade union. Local licensees claimed compensation for the war either curtailing or ruining their businesses. A glut of rabbits appeared on Cambridge dinner tables prompting a local poet and wit to write:

Rabbits young and rabbits old
Rabbits hot and rabbits cold
Rabbits tender, rabbits tough,
The Lord be praised, I've had enough!

Rabbit has quite a strong taste and, although it was the staple diet of poachers and poor folk, it has largely gone out of fashion in the twenty-first century.

The university Tripos lists were very badly hit by the war. They were euphemistically described as 'thin Tripos lists'. In the maths Tripos, there were only three Indians and one Welshman, the lowest number since its foundation in 1747. There were three students in the classics Tripos, five candidates for the history Tripos, natural sciences had just

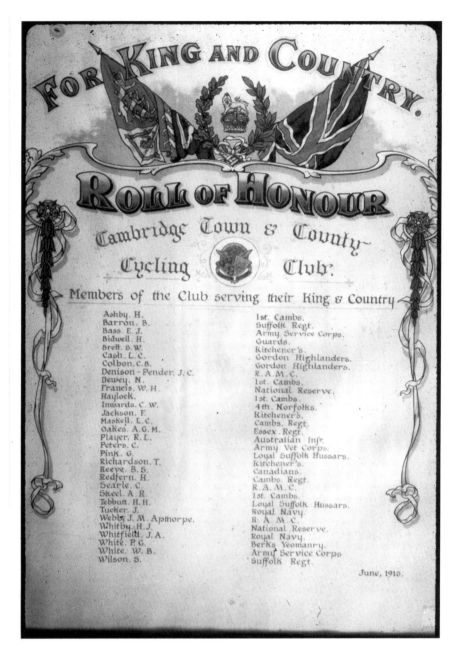

*Roll of Honour, Cambridge Town and Country Cycling Club, WW1
(courtesy of Cambridge Local Studies)*

twelve students instead of the usual 150, and the theology Tripos had four names instead of forty. The future of the university was seriously discussed and it was becoming accepted that it would never be the same again as it was before the war. Although not particularly interested in industrial problems, the university nevertheless recognised that young people would be needed post-war to rebuild trade and the economy and that extension of educational faculties and facilities would see new blood. Fears were expressed that Cambridge was 'growing stale'. In the past the town had been 'notorious for the production of slackness', although it was felt that to some extent 'the climate was responsible'. It wasn't that Cambridge people were not looking for mental challenge or change and progress but they were curtailed by rationing and restriction of transport facilities. 'Staleness is growing,' remarked one newspaper, while another wrote, 'although there is still determination to win the war there is a marked decline in readiness to give voluntary assistance to the war effort and lethargy seems to be growing.' On a more positive note, however, Cambridge boy scouts were working hard. Leave of absence from 14 July for one month was granted for 100 of them to work at flax pulling. It was war work of national importance, but it was not regular employment. Linen used for military purposes was manufactured from flax. The scouts also collected waste paper and raised £530 (£23,055), which Cambridge donated to the National Relief Fund.

Reading had also grown in popularity and the number of books borrowed from Cambridge libraries had greatly increased during the war. There were also appeals for books for troops in Red Cross hospitals and for soldiers at the front. The free libraries, *Dickens' great free schools*, were very popular and books provided a useful distraction from the grind of daily life. In Cambridge, Chinese cookery, making great use of cabbages, and cooking using a hay-box, were being advocated. Hay-box cooking was very slow but thorough, and a fuel saver. Folk were asked to save sun-dried fruit stones and hard nutshells for special war purposes.

America had finally entered the war in April 1917 and the American president, Woodrow Wilson, received an honorary degree from the university in the spring of 1918. American servicemen were now stationed in the town and county, and celebrated the 'glorious 4th' (of July), which commemorated the American Declaration of Independence on 4 July 1776.

There was a special intercessionary service held on 4 August at Great St Mary's to mark the fourth anniversary of the war and a large open-air service was held on Parker's Piece (which had been cleaned up along with Petersfield and Donkey's Common) in the evening. The Cambridge Regiment had captured 300 prisoners and thirty-three guns. One family celebrated that its six fighting sons were home for a family reunion. Nine hundred men from the Leys School alone were serving with the colours. Conscientious objectors were still a serious problem, however, who caused much anger and resentment. Queen Mary's Auxiliary Corps urgently required women in the Eastern Command to release the men to fight overseas. There were calls for clerks, cooks, waitresses and drivers. Although the need for more fighting men was as urgent as ever, the last phase of the war had finally begun.

At the end of August there was a heatwave and Cambridge citizens enjoyed picnics and relaxation in the sunshine. Bacon and beetroot salad or cottage cheese and cabbage salad were popular. The harvest was now in full swing. Female workers and schoolboys were bringing in 'a good crop of wheat, a satisfactory crop of oats and a variable crop of barley'. The Hundred Days Offensive had started on 8 August, and there was a sense of change in the air. There was news of victories, although 'conditions at the front still made the flesh creep'. Cambridge folk were taking holidays on a pre-war scale despite resentment from those who had to remain working on the war effort.

A 'charming garden fête' was held at Shelford. First Eastern arranged a 'capital programme' of bank holiday sports. Cambridge girl guides organised a challenge cup competition. There was a 'pretty' Fulbourn pageant. Land and water 'gymkhana frolic and sport' were held at Trinity College, and there were airmen's sports at Fowlmere, which included running, tug-of-war, and pillow-fighting on a pole. On a more serious note a large volunteers' camp was held at Madingley. Sausages, bacon and goat meat were no longer on ration, although one Cambridge citizen said that cooking bacon now was 'similar to cooking rhinoceros'.

Comrades Memorial Service and War Shrine, Ely 16 November 1919
(courtesy of Cambridge Local Studies)

American salt bacon was best used in haricot bean and bacon dishes. There were plenty of Norwegian herrings available and stocks of Greek currants had arrived. Surplus potatoes were also available.

However, as summer slowly turned to autumn and the end of the 'long vac', both town and gown experienced 'a time of dread and leanness'. The Stourbridge Fair, held in Barnwell at the end of September, went the way of Reach Fair and was gone with the war. Coal rationing was firmly in force and a hard winter was forecast.

Several cases of flu were being reported in the town. There was much excited talk on the Home Front of the forthcoming general election. It had taken longer than expected to prepare the new registers, and the election was postponed from November to December. The Labour Party was criticised for 'defection' in announcing that the Reverend Rhondda Williams might stand in opposition. It had been hoped that MPs would be returned unopposed, especially in the new county divisions. In the town the Conservative MP, Sir Eric Geddes, and the Liberal MP, Mr E.S. Montagu, hoped to be returned unopposed. And the two university representatives, Professor Sir Joseph Larmor and Mr Rawlinson, faced opposition from one Labour and one Independent candidate. The *Cambridge Chronicle* came out in support of David Lloyd George, the Liberal prime minister. There was doubt and debate on the 'female effect' in the university, although the government were trying to woo female voters with a series of measures aimed at working mothers and childcare.

The first Cambridge war shrine was unveiled at St Mary-the-Less. It had been subscribed by 124 members of the congregation and was blessed on the 566th anniversary of the church's dedication. A memorial service was held for the fallen men of Cambridge and the Isle of Ely in Great St Mary's at the end of September, a time of sad remembrance, but there was good progress in fighting on the Western Front. Finally, on 8 October, at the second Battle of Cambrai, the British finally broke through the Hindenburg Line. It was the beginning of the end.

There were numerous reports of German morale weakening as they steadily lost ground and growing demands in Britain for the punishment of Germany and its citizens. Germany was ready to sign an armistice for peace, but President Wilson was urged that any peace initiatives must take account of Germany's culpability by acknowledging fourteen points:

- responsibility for the war
- invasion of Belgium
- treatment of Belgian civilians
- Zeppelin raids

- bombardment of Serbia
- submarine campaign to sink shipping
- 'war crime' of the murders of Nurse Edith Cavell and Captain Fryatt
- attacks on hospital ships
- introduction of poison gas
- illegal deportation of French and Belgian citizens
- treatment of prisoners-of-war
- deliberate destruction of an occupied country
- complicity in the Armenian massacres
- treatment of Russia

Finally, on 11 November, came the news the whole country had waited over four years to hear: the immortal words of David Lloyd George 'at the eleventh minute of the eleventh hour of the eleventh month' when he told the nation that 'this morning came to end the cruellest and most terrible War that has ever scourged mankind. I hope we may say that thus, this fateful morning, came an end to all wars' hostilities ceased and the Great War came to an end'. Cambridge went crazy as the clouds of war lifted and there was 'rampant enthusiasm and great rejoicing'. A thanksgiving service was held in Great St Mary's, although the bells could not be rung due to damage caused by someone smashing open the belfry door in their excitement. The enormous losses had created a bond that broke down class barriers, and debutantes, shop girls and land workers hugged each other. Many cried with joy and relief. Huge crowds gathered in the town centre and there was music and dancing in the still darkened streets. Effigies of the kaiser were paraded through the town and ceremoniously burned.

Town, gown and county had survived all the grief, hardships, deprivations and changes. Now they believed they could rebuild a golden future.

Great War memorial, Cambridge

Index